To Dan

On her graduation day. The best and the worst of America in one book. to remind her of Maine and us.

Love,

Marsh

101

GREAT
POEMS
★ OF ★
AMERICA

CB
CONTEMPORARY
BOOKS

101 great poems of America.
    p.   cm.
    ISBN 0-8092-3927-2
    1. American poetry.   I. Contemporary Books,
inc.   II. Title: One hundred and one great poems of
America.   III. Title: One hundred and one great
poems of America.
PS586.A15   1992
811.008—dc20   91-29725
                                                       CIP

Acknowledgments

"America Befriend" and "America for Me" by Henry Van Dyke. Courtesy of Charles Scribner's Sons.

"America the Beautiful" from *Poems* by Katharine Lee Bates. All rights reserved. Reprinted by permission of the publisher, E. P. Dutton, a division of New American Library.

"Lift Every Voice and Sing" by James W. Johnson. Used by permission of Edward B. Marks Music Company.

"The People's Prayer" by Amos R. Wells. Used by permission of the International Society of Christian Endeavor.

"November 1918" by Joseph Mills Hanson. Reprinted courtesy of *Stars and Stripes*.

"Shine, Republic." Copyright © 1934 and renewed 1962 by Donnan Jeffers and Gartch Jeffers. Reprinted from *The Selected Poetry of Robinson Jeffers*, by Robinson Jeffers, by permission of Random House, Inc.

"I, Too." Copyright © 1926 by Alfred A. Knopf, Inc., and renewed 1954 by Langston Hughes. Reprinted from *Selected Poems of Langston Hughes*, by Langston Hughes, by permission of the publisher.

"The Soldier" by Robert Frost. From *The Poetry of Robert Frost*, edited by Edward Connery Lathem. Copyright 1928, © 1969 by Holt, Rinehart and Winston. Copyright © 1956 by Robert Frost. Reprinted by permission of Henry Holt and Company.

"American Names" by Stephen Vincent Benét. From *Ballads and Poems: 1915-1930* by Stephen Vincent Benét. Copyright 1931 by Stephen Vincent Benét. Copyright © 1959 by Rosemary Carr Benét. Reprinted by permission of Henry Holt and Company, Inc.

"The Gift Outright" by Robert Frost. From *The Poetry of Robert Frost*, edited by Edward Connery Lathem. Copyright 1942 by Robert Frost. Copyright © 1969 by Holt, Rinehart and Winston. Copyright © 1970 by Lesley Frost Ballantine. Reprinted by permission of Henry Holt and Company, Inc..

"Plain-Chant for America" from *Plain-Chant for America: Poems and Ballads by Katherine Garrison Chapin*. Copyright 1938, 1939 by Katherine Garrison Chapin Biddle. By permission of Harper & Row, Publishers, Inc.

Specified extract from "The Columbiad" by Joel Barlow and "A Poem on the Industry of the United States of America" by David Humphreys in *The Connecticut Wits*: Edited with an Introduction by Vernon Louis Parrington (Thomas Y. Crowell Co.) Harper & Row. By permission of Harper & Row, Publishers, Inc.

"Cool Tombs" by Carl Sandburg. From *Cornhuskers* by Carl Sandburg, copyright 1918 by Holt, Rinehart and Winston, Inc.; renewed 1946 by Carl Sandburg. Reprinted by permission of Harcourt Brace Jovanovich, Inc.

America for Me

HENRY VAN DYKE
(1852–1933)

'Tis fine to see the Old World, and travel up and down
Among the famous palaces and cities of renown,
To admire the crumbly castles and the statues of the
    kings,—
But now I think I've had enough of antiquated things.

> *So it's home again, and home again, America for me!*
> *My heart is turning home again, and there I long to*
> * be,*
> *In the land of youth and freedom beyond the ocean*
> * bars,*
> *Where the air is full of sunlight and the flag is full of*
> * stars.*

Oh, London is a man's town, there's power in the air;
And Paris is a woman's town, with flowers in her hair;
And it's sweet to dream in Venice, and it's great to
    study Rome;
But when it comes to living there is no place like home.

I like the German fir-woods, in green battalions
    drilled;
I like the gardens of Versailles with flashing fountains
    filled;
But, oh, to take your hand, my dear, and ramble for a
    day
In the friendly western woodland where Nature has
    her way!

I know that Europe's wonderful, yet something seems
    to lack:
The Past is too much with her, and the people looking
    back.

But the glory of the Present is to make the Future
    free,—
We love our land for what she is and what she is to be.

Oh, it's home again, and home again, America for
    me!
I want a ship that's westward bound to plough the
    rolling sea,
To the blessed Land of Room Enough beyond the
    ocean bars,
Where the air is full of sunlight and the flag is full of
    stars.

My People Came to This Country
STRUTHERS BURT
(1882–1954)

My people came to this country
In need of a land that was free,
So I think the only thing I can do,
If a decent man I would be,
Is to walk with my head held high and proud
For the blood that runs in me.

My people came to this country
—And the seas were a green great space—
Because the trees were kind and tall
And the fields a pleasant place,
And brave men worshipped as they would
And thought with an open face.

Beat in memory ancient drums
Like the throbbing of a vein;
Wave on the winds of a continent
Ragged flags in the rain,
For the ghosts of countless countrymen
Are on the march again.

My people came to this country
With dreams too quick for hate;
A neighbor was a light in the dark
Or a hand upon a gate,
And whence he came was no news at all
In the building of a state.

Now God bless every stick of it
And every path and post;
The broad slow rivers of the south,
The quick bright streams of the frost,
And the mountains like a mighty oath
That does not count the cost.

And God bless all the dipping fields
From the mountains to the sea,
And grant that I walk like a fearless man
For the blood that runs in me.

Land That We Love

Richard Watson Gilder
(1844–1909)

Land that we love! Thou Future of the World!
Thou refuge of the noble heart oppressed!
Oh, never by thy shining image hurled
From its high place in the adoring breast
Of him who worships thee with jealous love!
Keep thou thy starry forehead as the dove
All white, and to the eternal Dawn inclined!
Thou art not for thyself but for mankind,
And to despair of thee were to despair
Of man, of man's high destiny, of God!
Of thee should man despair, the journey trod
Upward, through unknown eons, stair on stair,
By this our race, with bleeding feet and slow,
Were but the pathway to a darker woe
Than yet was visioned by the heavy heart
Of prophet. To despair of thee! Ah no!
For thou thyself art Hope, Hope of the World thou
art!

3

America

ARLO BATES
(1850–1918)

For, O America, our country!—land
    Hid in the west through centuries, till men
Through countless tyrannies could understand
    The priceless worth of freedom,—once again
The world was new-created when thy shore
    First knew the Pilgrim keels, the one last test
The race might make of manhood, nor give o'er
    The strife with evil till it proved its best.
Thy true sons stand as torch-bearers, to hold
    A guiding light. Here the last stand is made.
Of we fail here, what new Columbus bold,
    Steering brave prow through black seas unafraid,
Finds out a fresh land where man may abide
    And freedom yet be saved? The whole round earth
Has seen the battle fought. Where shall men hide
    From tyranny and wrong, where life have worth,
If here the cause succumb? If greed of gold
    Or lust of power or falsehood triumph here,
The race is lost! A globe dispeopled, cold,
    Rolled down the void a voiceless, lifeless sphere,
Were not so stamped by all which hope debars
    As were this earth, plunging along through space
Conquered by evil, shamed among the stars,
    Bearing a base, enslaved, dishonored race!
Here has the battle its last vantage ground;
    Here all is won, or here must all be lost;
Here freedom's trumpets one last rally sound;
    Here to the breeze its blood-stained flag is tossed.
America, last hope of man and truth,
    The name must through all coming ages be
The badge unspeakable of shame and ruth,
    Or glorious pledge that man through truth is free.
This is thy destiny; the choice is thine
    To lead all nations and outshine them all;—
But if thou failest, deeper shame is thine,
    And none shall spare to mock thee in thy fall.

A Toast to Our Native Land

ROBERT BRIDGES

(1844–1930)

Huge and alert, irascible yet strong,
We make our fitful way 'mid right and wrong.
One time we pour out millions to be free,
Then rashly sweep an empire from the sea!
One time we strike the shackles from the slaves,
And then, quiescent, we are ruled by knaves.
Often we rudely break restraining bars,
And confidently reach out toward the stars.

Yet under all there flows a hidden stream
Sprung from the Rock of Freedom, the great dream
Of Washington and Franklin, men of old
Who knew that Freedom is not bought with gold.
This is the Land we love, our heritage,
Strange mixture of the gross and fine, yet sage
And full of promise—destined to be great.
Drink to Our Native Land! God Bless the State!

Columbus

JOAQUIN MILLER

(1841–1913)

Behind him lay the gray Azores,
   Behind the Gates of Hercules;
Before him not the ghost of shores,
   Before him only shoreless seas.
The good mate said: "Now must we pray,
   For lo! the very stars are gone.
Brave Adm'r'l, speak; what shall I say?"
   "Why, say: 'Sail on ! sail on! and on!' "

"My men grow mutinous day by day;
   My men grow ghastly wan and weak."
The stout mate thought of home; a spray
   Of salt wave washed his swarthy cheek.
"What shall I say, brave Adm'r'l, say,
   If we sight naught but seas at dawn?"
"Why, you shall say, at break of day:
   'Sail on! sail on! sail on! and on!' "

They sailed and sailed, as winds might blow,
   Until at last the blanched mate said:
"Why, now not even God would know
   Should I and all my men fall dead.
These very winds forget their way,
   For God from these dread seas is gone.
Now speak, brave Adm'r'l; speak and say"—
   He said: "Sail on! sail on! and on!"

They sailed. They sailed. Then spake the mate:
   "This mad sea shows his teeth to-night;
He curls his lips, he lies in wait,
   With lifted teeth, as if to bite;
Brave Adm'r'l, say but one good word;
   What shall we do when hope is gone?"
The words leapt like a leaping sword:
   "Sail on! sail on! sail on! and on!"

Then, pale and worn, he kept his deck,
   And peered through darkness. Ah, that night
Of all dark nights! And then a speck—
   A light! a light! a light! a light!
It grew, a starlit flag unfurled!
   It grew to be Time's burst of dawn.
He gained a world; he gave that world
   Its grandest lesson: "On! sail on!"

Atlantic Charter: 1942

FRANCIS BRETT YOUNG

(1884–1954)

What were you carrying, Pilgrims, Pilgrims?
What did you carry beyond the sea?
   We carried the Book, we carried the Sword,
   A steadfast heart in the fear of the Lord,
   And a living faith in His plighted word
   That all men should be free.

What were your memories, Pilgrims, Pilgrims?
What of the dreams you bore away?
   We carried the songs our fathers sung
   By the hearths of home when they were young,
   And the comely words of the mother-tongue
   In which they learnt to pray.

What did you find there, Pilgrims, Pilgrims?
What did you find beyond the waves?
   A stubborn land and a barren shore,
   Hunger and want and sickness sore:
   All these we found and gladly bore
   Rather than be slaves.

How did you fare there, Pilgrims, Pilgrims?
What did you build in that stubborn land?
   We felled the forest and tilled the sod
   Of a continent no man had trod
And we established there, in the Grace of God,
The rights whereby we stand.

What are you bringing us, Pilgrims, Pilgrims?
Bringing us back in this bitter day?
   The selfsame things we carried away:
   The Book, the Sword,
   The fear of the Lord,
   And the boons our fathers dearly bought:
   Freedom of Worship, Speech and Thought,
   Freedom from Want, Freedom from Fear,
   The liberties we hold most dear,
   And who shall say us Nay?

Pocahontas
January 5, 1608

WILLIAM MAKEPEACE THACKERAY
(1811–1863)

Wearied arm and broken sword
   Wage in vain the desperate fight;
Round him press a countless horde,
   He is but a single knight.
Hark! a cry of triumph shrill
   Through the wilderness resounds,
   As, with twenty bleeding wounds,
Sinks the warrior, fighting still.

Now they heap the funeral pyre,
   And the torch of death they light;
Ah! 'tis hard to die by fire!
   Who will shield the captive knight?
Round the stake with fiendish cry
   Wheel and dance the savage crowd,
   Cold the victim's mien and proud,
And his breast is bared to die.

Who will shield the fearless heart?
   Who avert the murderous blade?
From the throng with sudden start
   See, there springs an Indian maid.
Quick she stands before the knight:
   "Loose the chain, unbind the ring!
   I am daughter of the king,
And I claim the Indian right!"

Dauntlessly aside she flings
   Lifted axe and thirsty knife,
Fondly to his heart she clings,
   And her bosom guards his life!
In the woods of Powhatan,
   Still 'tis told by Indian fires
   How a daughter of their sires
Saved a captive Englishman.

The Landing of the Pilgrim Fathers in New England

FELICIA D. HEMANS

(1793–1835)

The breaking waves dashed high
  On a stern and rock-bound coast,
And the woods against a stormy sky
  Their giant branches tossed;

And the heavy night hung dark
  The hills and waters o'er,
When a band of exiles moored their bark
  On the wild New England shore.

Not as the conqueror comes,
  They, the true-hearted, came;
Not with the roll of the stirring drums,
  And the trumpet that sings of fame:

Not as the flying come,
  In silence and in fear;
They shook the depths of the desert gloom
  And their hymns of lofty cheer.

Amidst the storm they sang,
  And the stars heard, and the sea;
And the sounding aisles of the dim woods rang
  To the anthem of the free.

The ocean eagle soared
  From his nest by the white wave's foam,
And the rocking pines of the forest roared,—
  This was their welcome home.

There were men with hoary hair
  Amidst that pilgrim-band:
Why had they come to wither there,
  Away from their childhood's land?

There was woman's fearless eye,
  Lit by her deep love's truth;
There was manhood's brow serenely high,
  And the fiery heart of youth.

What sought they thus afar?
  Bright jewels of the mine?
The wealth of seas, the spoils of war?—
  They sought a faith's pure shrine!

Ay, call it holy ground,
  The soil where first they trod;
They have left unstained what there they found,—
  Freedom to worship God.

Lafayette to Washington
From *Valley Forge*
MAXWELL ANDERSON
(1888–1959)

Lafayette to Washington:
    Shall I begin by saying
some things you know, but may have forgotten? This
    world
you have cut from the wilderness, is a new world,
    brighter
with sun in summer, colder with winter cold
than the world I knew. The air's strange-sharp, the
    voice
rings here with a hard ring. I find no man
but looks you in the eye and says his thought
in your teeth, and means it. This was not known before
on this star we inhabit. Europe has thirty kings
and a hundred million slaves. But here in this land
each man is a king and walks like a king, each woman
bears herself regally, like a queen. You will find
this is not easy to throw away. The air
of this coast has fired your blood and while three
    among you,
no more than three, hold hard against the old masters,
the kingdoms lessen and dwindle. They've felt your
    breath
and feared it, in the old world. Lose! now the gods
in heaven hear me, you cannot lose! Bow down
and humble yourselves if you can! It's not in you to
    bow
nor to speak humbly. It's a trick you've never learned
and cannot learn in this air!—As for these thrones
that men have bowed to, I've come from them lately
    and seen them,
how they're eaten down with old vices and slimed with
    worms
'til they crumble into moats! Lower your muzzles,
droop your flags! Even so the kingdoms falter
and go down of themselves!

Liberty Tree

THOMAS PAINE

(1737–1809)

In a chariot of light from the regions of day,
  The Goddess of Liberty came;
Ten thousand celestials directed the way
  And hither conducted the dame.
A fair budding branch from the gardens above,
  Where millions with millions agree,
She brought in her hand as a pledge of her love,
  And the plant she named *Liberty Tree*.

The celestial exotic struck deep in the ground,
  Like a native it flourished and bore;
The fame of its fruit drew the nations around,
  To seek out this peaceable shore.
Unmindful of names or distinction they came,
  For freemen like brothers agree;
With one spirit endued, they one friendship pursued,
  And their temple was *Liberty Tree*.

Beneath this fair tree, like the patriarchs of old,
  Their bread in contentment they ate,
Unvexed with the troubles of silver and gold,
  The cares of the grand and the great.
With timber and tar they Old England supplied,
  And supported her power on the sea;
Her battles they fought, without getting a groat,
  For the honor of *Liberty Tree*.

But hear, O ye swains, 'tis a tale most profane,
  How all the tyrannical powers,
Kings, Commons, and Lords, are uniting amain
  To cut down this guardian of ours;
From the east to the west blow the trumpet to arms
  Through the land let the sound of it flee,
Let the far and the near, all unite with a cheer,
  In defence of our *Liberty Tree*.

Betsy's Battle-Flag

Minna Irving
(1872–?)

From dusk till dawn the livelong night
She kept the tallow dips alight,
And fast her nimble fingers flew
To sew the stars upon the blue.
With weary eyes and aching head
She stitched the stripes of white and red,
And when the day came up the stair
Complete across a carven chair
  Hung Betsy's battle-flag.

Like shadows in the evening gray
The Continentals filed away,
With broken boots and ragged coats,
But hoarse defiance in their throats;
They bore the marks of want and cold,
And some were lame and some were old,
And some with wounds untended bled,
But floating bravely overhead
    Was Betsy's battle-flag.

When fell the battle's leaden rain,
The soldier hushed his moans of pain
And raised his dying head to see
King George's troopers turn and flee.
Their charging column reeled and broke,
And vanished in the rolling smoke,
Before the glory of the stars,
The snowy stripes, and scarlet bars
    Of Betsy's battle-flag.

The simple stone of Betsy Ross
Is covered now with mould and moss,
But still her deathless banner flies,
And keeps the color of the skies.
A nation thrills, a nation bleeds,
A nation follows where it leads,
And every man is proud to yield
His life upon a crimson field
    For Betsy's battle-flag!

The American Patriot's Prayer
1776

AUTHOR UNKNOWN

Parent of all, omnipotent
   In heav'n, and earth below,
Thro' all creation's bounds unspent,
   Whose streams of goodness flow.

Teach me to know from whence I rose,
   And unto what design'd;
No private aims let me propose,
   Since link'd with human kind.

But chief to hear my country's voice,
   May all my thoughts incline,
'T is reason's law, 't is virtue's choice,
   'T is nature's call and thine.

Me from fair freedom's sacred cause
   Let nothing e'er divide;
Grandeur, nor gold, nor vain applause,
   Nor friendship false misguide.

Let me not faction's partial hate
   Pursue to *this land's* woe;
Nor grasp the thunder of the state
   To wound a private foe.

If, for the right, to wish the wrong
   My country shall combine,
Single to serve th' erron'ous throng,
   Spite of themselves, be mine.

Paul Revere's Ride

HENRY WADSWORTH LONGFELLOW

(1807–1882)

Listen, my children, and you shall hear
Of the midnight ride of Paul Revere,
On the eighteenth of April, in Seventy-five;
Hardly a man is now alive
Who remembers that famous day and year.

He said to his friend, "If the British march
By land or sea from the town to-night,
Hang a lantern aloft in the belfry arch
Of the North Church tower as a signal light,—
One if by land, and two if by sea;
And I on the opposite shore will be,
Ready to ride and spread the alarm
Through every Middlesex village and farm,
For the country folk to be up and to arm."

Then he said "Good-night!" and with muffled oar
Silently rowed to the Charlestown shore,
Just as the moon rose over the bay,
Where swinging wide at her moorings lay
The *Somerset*, British man-of-war;
A phantom ship, with each mast and spar
Across the moon like a prison bar,
And a huge black hulk, that was magnified
By its own reflection in the tide.

Meanwhile, his friend through alley and street
Wanders and watches, with eager ears,
Till in the silence around him he hears
The muster of men at the barrack door,
The sound of arms, and the tramp of feet,
And the measured tread of the grenadiers,
Marching down to their boats on the shore.

Then he climbed the tower of the Old North Church,
By the wooden stairs, with stealthy tread,
To the belfry chamber overhead,

And startled the pigeons from their perch
On the sombre rafters, that round him made
Masses and moving shapes of shade,—
By the trembling ladder, steep and tall,
To the highest window in the wall,
Where he paused to listen and look down
A moment on the roofs of the town
And the moonlight flowing over all.

Beneath, in the churchyard, lay the dead,
In their night encampment on the hill,
Wrapped in silence so deep and still
That he could hear, like a sentinel's tread,
The watchful night-wind, as it went
Creeping along from tent to tent,
And seeming to whisper, "All is well!"
A moment only he feels the spell
Of the place and the hour, and the secret dread
Of the lonely belfry and the dead;
For suddenly all his thoughts are bent
On a shadowy something far away,
Where the river widens to meet the bay,—
A line of black that bends and floats
On the rising tide like a bridge of boats.

Meanwhile, impatient to mount and ride,
Booted and spurred, with a heavy stride
On the opposite shore walked Paul Revere.
Now he patted his horse's side,
Now he gazed at the landscape far and near,
Then, impetuous, stamped the earth,
And turned and tightened his saddle girth;
But mostly he watched with eager search
The belfry tower of the Old North Church,
As it rose above the graves on the hill,
Lonely and spectral and sombre and still.
And lo! as he looks, on the belfry's height
A glimmer, and then a gleam of light!
He springs to the saddle, the bridle he turns,
But lingers and gazes, till full on his sight
A second lamp in the belfry burns.

A hurry of hoofs in a village street,
A shape in the moonlight, a bulk in the dark,
And beneath, from the pebbles, in passing, a spark
Struck out by a steed flying fearless and fleet;
That was all! And yet, through the gloom and the
    light,
The fate of a nation was riding that night,
And the spark struck out by that steed, in his flight,
Kindled the land into flame with its heat.
He has left the village and mounted the steep,
And beneath him, tranquil and broad and deep,
Is the Mystic, meeting the ocean tides;
And under the alders that skirt its edge,
Now soft on the sand, now loud on the ledge,
Is heard the tramp of his steed as he rides.

It was twelve by the village clock
When he crossed the bridge into Medford town.
He heard the crowing of the cock,
And the barking of the farmer's dog,
And felt the damp of the river fog,
That rises after the sun goes down.

It was one by the village clock,
When he galloped into Lexington.
He saw the gilded weathercock
Swim in the moonlight as he passed,
And the meeting-house windows, black and bare,
Gaze at him with a spectral glare,
As if they already stood aghast
At the bloody work they would look upon.

It was two by the village clock,
When he came to the bridge in Concord town.
He heard the bleating of the flock,
And the twitter of birds among the trees,
And felt the breath of the morning breeze
Blowing over the meadow brown.
And one was safe and asleep in his bed
Who at the bridge would be first to fall,
Who that day would be lying dead,
Pierced by a British musket ball.

You know the rest. In the books you have read
How the British Regulars fired and fled,—
How the farmers gave them ball for ball,
From behind each fence and farmyard wall,
Chasing the redcoats down the lane,
Then crossing the fields to emerge again
Under the trees at the turn of the road,
And only pausing to fire and load.

So through the night rode Paul Revere;
And so through the night went his cry of alarm
To every Middlesex village and farm,—
A cry of defiance, and not of fear,
A voice in the darkness, a knock at the door,
And a word that shall echo for evermore!
For, borne on the night-wind of the Past,
Through all our history, to the last,
In the hour of darkness and peril and need,
The people will waken and listen to hear
The hurrying hoof-beats of that steed,
And the midnight message of Paul Revere.

The War Inevitable, March, 1775

PATRICK HENRY

(1736–1799)

They tell us, Sir, that we are weak—unable to cope with so formidable an adversary. But when shall we be stronger? Will it be the next week, or the next year? Will it be when we are totally disarmed, and when a British guard shall be stationed in every house? Shall we gather strength by irresolution and inaction? Shall we acquire the means of effectual resistance by lying supinely on our backs, and hugging the delusive phantom of hope, until our enemies shall have bound us hand and foot? Sir, we are not weak, if we make a proper use of those means which the God of nature hath placed in our power.

Three millions of People, armed in the holy cause of liberty, and in such a country as that which we possess, are invincible by any force which our enemy can send against us. Beside, Sir, we shall not fight our battles alone. There is a just God who presides over the destinies of Nations, and who will raise up friends to fight our battles for us. The battle, Sir, is not to the strong alone; it is to the vigilant, the active, the brave. Besides, Sir, we have no election. If we were base enough to desire it, it is now too late to retire from the contest. There is no retreat but in submission and slavery! Our chains are forged! Their clanking may be heard on the plains of Boston! The war is inevitable; and let it come! I repeat, Sir, let it come!

It is in vain, Sir, to extenuate the matter. Gentlemen may cry, Peace, Peace!—but there is no peace. The war is actually begun! The next gale that sweeps from the North will bring to our ears the clash of resounding arms! Our brethren are already in the field! Why stand we here idle? What is it that Gentlemen wish? What would they have? Is life so dear, or peace so sweet, as to be purchased at the price

of chains and slavery? Forbid it, Almighty God! I know
not what course others may take; but as for me, give
me liberty or give me death!

Nathan Hale
William Ordway Partridge

One hero dies,—a thousand new ones rise,
   As flowers are sown where perfect blossoms fall,—
Then quite unknown,—the name of Hale now cries
   Where duty sounds her silent call;

With head erect he moves, and stately pace,
   To meet an awful doom,—no ribald jest
Brings scorn or hate to that exalted face,
   His thoughts are far away, poised and at rest;

Now on the scaffold see him turn and bid
   Farewell to home and all his heart holds dear,
Majestic presence,—all men's weakness hid,
   And all his strength in that one hour made clear,—
"I have one last regret,—that is to give
But one poor life, that my own land may live!"

Independence Bell,
July 4, 1776

AUTHOR UNKNOWN

There was a tumult in the city
In the quaint old Quaker town,
And the streets were rife with people
Pacing restless up and down—
People gathering at corners,
Where they whispered each to each,
And the sweat stood on their temples
With the earnestness of speech.

As the bleak Atlantic currents
Lash the wild Newfoundland shore,
So they beat against the State House,
So they surged against the door;
And the mingling of their voices
Made the harmony profound,
Till the quiet street of Chestnut
Was all turbulent with sound.

"Will they do it?" "Dare they do it?"
"Who is speaking?" "What's the news?"
"What of Adams?" "What of Sherman?"
"Oh, God grant they won't refuse!"
"Make some way there!" "Let me nearer!"
"I am stifling!" "Stifle then!
When a nation's life's at hazard,
We've no time to think of men!"

So they surged against the State House,
While all solemnly inside,
Sat the Continental Congress,
Truth and reason for their guide,
O'er a simple scroll debating,
Which, though simple it might be,
Yet should shake the cliffs of England
With the thunders of the free.

Far aloft in that high steeple
Sat the bellman, old and gray,
He was weary of the tyrant
And his iron-sceptered sway;
So he sat, with one hand ready
On the clapper of the bell,
When his eye could catch the signal,
The long-expected news to tell.

See! See! The dense crowd quivers
Through all its lengthy line,
As the boy beside the portal
Hastens forth to give the sign!
With his little hands uplifted,
Breezes dallying with his hair,
Hark! with deep, clear intonation,
Breaks his young voice on the air.

Hushed the people's swelling murmur,
Whilst the boy crys joyously;
"Ring!" he shouts, "Ring! Grandpapa,
Ring! oh, ring for Liberty!"
Quickly, at the given signal
The old bellman lifts his hand,
Forth he sends the goods news, making
Iron music through the land.

How they shouted! What rejoicing!
How the old bell shook the air,
Till the clang of freedom ruffled,
The calmly gliding Delaware!
How the bonfires and the torches

Lighted up the night's repose,
And from the flames, like fabled Phoenix,
Our glorious liberty arose!

That old State House bell is silent,
Hushed is now its clamorous tongue;
But the spirit it awakened
Still is living—ever young;
And when we greet the smiling sunlight
On the fourth of each July,
We will ne'er forget the bellman
Who, betwixt the earth and sky,
Rung out, loudly, "Independence";
Which, please God, shall never die!

The Declaration of Independence
In Congress, July 4th, 1776
The Unanimous Declaration of the Thirteen United States of America

When, in the course of human events, it becomes necessary for one people to dissolve the political bands which have connected them with another, and to assume, among the powers of the earth, the separate and equal station to which the laws of nature and of nature's God entitle them, a decent respect to the opinions of mankind requires that they should declare the causes which impel them to the separation.

We hold these truths to be self-evident: that all men are created equal; that they are endowed by their Creator with certain inalienable rights; that among these are life, liberty, and the pursuit of happiness. That to secure these rights, governments are instituted among men, deriving their just powers from the consent of the governed; that whenever any form of government becomes destructive of these ends it is the right of the people to alter or to abolish it, and to institute a new government, laying its foundation on such principles, and organizing its powers in such form, as to them shall seem most likely to effect their safety and happiness. Prudence, indeed, will dictate, that governments long established should not be changed for light and transient causes; and accordingly all experience hath shown, that mankind are more disposed to suffer, while evils are sufferable, than to right themselves by abolishing the forms to which they are accustomed. But when a long train of abuses and usurpations, pursuing invariably the same object, evinces a design to reduce them under absolute despotism, it is their right, it is their duty, to throw off such government, and to provide new guards for their future security. Such has been the patient sufferance of these colonies; and such is now the necessity which constrains them to alter their former system of government. The history of the present king of Great Britain is a history of repeated injuries and usurpations, all having in direct object the establishment of an absolute tyranny over these states. To prove this, let facts be submitted to a candid world.

He has refused his assent to laws the most wholesome and necessary for the public good.

He has forbidden his governors to pass laws of immediate and pressing importance, unless suspended in their operation till his assent should be obtained; and when so suspended, he has utterly neglected to attend to them.

He has refused to pass other laws for the accommodation of large districts of people, unless those people would relinquish the right of representation in the legislature—a right inestimable to them, and formidable to tyrants only.

He has called together legislative bodies at places unusual, uncomfortable, and distant from the depository of their public records, for the sole purpose of fatiguing them into compliance with his measures.

He has dissolved representative houses repeatedly, for opposing, with manly firmness, his invasions on the rights of the people.

He has refused, for a long time after such dissolutions, to cause others to be elected; whereby the legislative powers, incapable of annihilation, have returned to the people at large, for their exercise, the state remaining in the meantime exposed to all the dangers of invasion from without, and convulsions within.

He has endeavored to prevent the population of these states; for that purpose obstructing the laws for naturalization of foreigners; refusing to pass others to encourage their migration hither, and raising the conditions of new appropriations of lands.

He has obstructed the administration of justice, by refusing his assent to laws for establishing judiciary powers.

He has made judges dependent on his will alone, for the tenure of their offices, and the amount and payment of their salaries.

He has erected a multitude of new offices, and sent hither swarms of officers, to harass our people, and eat out their substance.

He has kept among us, in times of peace, standing armies, without the consent of our legislature.

He has affected to render the military independent of, and superior to, the civil power.

He has combined with others to subject us to a jurisdiction foreign to our constitution, and unacknowledged by our laws; giving his assent to their acts of pretended legislation:

For quartering large bodies of armed troops among us:

For protecting them, by a mock trial, from punishment for any murders which they should commit on the inhabitants of these states:

For cutting off our trade with all parts of the world:

For imposing taxes on us without our consent:

For depriving us, in many cases, of the benefits of trial by jury:

For transporting us beyond seas to be tried for pretended offences:

For abolishing the free system of English laws in a neighboring province, establishing therein an arbitrary government, and enlarging its boundaries, so as to render it at once an example and fit instrument for introducing the same absolute rule into these colonies:

For taking away our charters, abolishing our most valuable laws, and altering, fundamentally, the forms of our governments:

For suspending our own legislatures, and declaring themselves invested with power to legislate for us in all cases whatsoever.

He has abdicated government here, by declaring us out of his protection and waging war against us.

He has plundered our seas, ravaged our coasts, burnt our towns and destroyed the lives of our people.

He is at this time transporting large armies of foreign mercenaries to complete the works of death, desolation, and tyranny, already begun with circumstances of cruelty and perfidy scarcely paralleled in the most barbarous ages, and totally unworthy the head of a civilized nation.

He has constrained our fellow-citizens, taken captive on the high seas, to bear arms against their country, to become the executioners of their friends and brethren, or to fall themselves by their hands.

He has excited domestic insurrections among us, and has endeavored to bring on the inhabitants of our frontiers the merciless Indian savages, whose known rule of warfare is an undistinguished destruction of all ages, sexes, and conditions.

In every stage of these oppressions we have petitioned for redress in the most humble terms; our repeated petitions have been answered only by repeated injury. A prince whose character is thus marked by every act which may define a tyrant is unfit to be the ruler of a free people.

Nor have we been wanting in attentions to our British brethren. We have warned them, from time to time, of attempts by their legislature to extend an unwarrantable jurisdiction over us. We have reminded them of the circumstances of our emigration and settlement here. We have appealed to their native justice and magnanimity, and we have conjured them by the ties of our common kindred to disavow these usurpations, which would inevitably interrupt our connections and correspondence. They, too, have been deaf to the voice of justice and consanguinity. We must, therefore, acquiesce in the necessity which denounces our separation, and hold them, as we hold the rest of mankind, enemies in war, in peace friends.

We, therefore, the representatives of the United States of America, in General Congress assembled, appealing to the Supreme Judge of the world for the rectitude of our intentions, do, in the name and by the authority of the good people of these colonies, solemnly publish and declare that these United Colonies are, and of right ought to be, free and independent States; that they are absolved from all allegiance to the British crown, and that all political connection between them and the State of Great Britain is, and ought to be, totally dissolved; and that, as free and independent States, they have full power to levy war, conclude peace, contract alliances, establish commerce, and to do all other acts and things which independent States may of right do. And for the support of this declaration, with a firm reliance on the protection of Divine Providence, we mutually pledge to each other our lives, our fortunes, and our sacred honor.

Signed by order and in behalf of the Congress.

The Columbiad
Excerpt
JOEL BARLOW
(1754–1812)

Based on its rock of Right your empire lies,
On walls of wisdom let the fabric rise;
Preserve your principles, their force unfold,
Let nations prove them and let kings behold.
EQUALITY, your first firm-grounded stand;
Then FREE ELECTION; then your FEDERAL BAND;
This holy Triad should forever shine
The great compendium of all rights divine,
Creed of all schools, whence youths by millions draw
Their themes of right, their decalogues of law;
Till men shall wonder (in these codes inured)
How wars were made, how tyrants were endured.
   Then shall your works of art superior rise,
Your fruits pefume a larger length of skies,
Canals careering climb your sunbright hills,
Vein the green slopes and strow their nurturing rills,
Thro tunnel'd heights and sundering ridges glide,
Rob the rich west of half Kenhawa's tide,
Mix your wide climates, all their stores confound,
And plant new ports in every midland mound.
Your lawless Mississippi, now who slimes
And drowns and desolates his waste of climes,
Ribb'd with your dikes, his torrent shall restrain,
And ask your leave to travel to the main;
Won from his wave while rising cantons smile,
Rear their glad nations and reward their toil.

Old Ironsides

Written with reference to the proposed
breaking up of the famous U.S. frigate
Constitution.

OLIVER WENDELL HOLMES
(1809–1894)

Ay, tear her tattered ensign down!
   Long has it waved on high,
And many an eye has danced to see
   That banner in the sky;
Beneath it rung the battle-shout,
   And burst the cannon's roar:
The meteor of the ocean air
   Shall sweep the clouds no more!

Her deck, once red with heroes' blood
   Where knelt the vanquished foe,
When winds were hurrying o'er the flood
   And waves were white below,
No more shall feel the victor's tread,
   Or know the conquered knee:
The harpies of the shore shall pluck
   The eagle of the sea!

O better that her shattered hulk
   Should sink beneath the wave!
Her thunders shook the mighty deep,
   And there should be her grave:
Nail to the mast her holy flag,
   Set every threadbare sail,
And give her to the god of storms,
   The lightning and the gale!

Preamble to the Constitution of the United States

We, the people of the United States, in order to form a more perfect union, establish justice, insure domestic tranquillity, provide for the common defence, promote the general welfare, and secure the blessings of liberty to ourselves and our posterity, do ordain and establish this CONSTITUTION for the United States of America.

I Hear America Singing
WALT WHITMAN
(1819–1892)

I hear America singing, the varied carols I hear,
Those of mechanics, each one singing his as it should
    be blithe and strong,
The carpenter singing his as he measures his plank or
    beam,
The mason singing as he makes ready for work, or
    leaves off work,
The boatman singing what belongs to him in his boat,
    the deckhand singing on the steamboat deck,
The shoemaker singing as he sits on his bench, the
    hatter singing as he stands,
The wood-cutter's song, the ploughboy's on his way in
    the morning, or at noon intermission or at
    sundown,
The delicious singing of the mother, or of the young
    wife at work, or of the girl sewing or washing,
Each singing what belongs to him or her and to none
    else,
The day what belongs to the day—at night the party of
    young fellows, robust, friendly,
Singing with open mouths their strong melodious
    songs.

American Names

STEPHEN VINCENT BENET
(1898–1943)

I have fallen in love with American names,
The sharp gaunt names that never get fat,
The snakeskin-titles of mining-claims,
The plumed war-bonnet of Medicine Hat,
Tucson and Deadwood and Lost Mule Flat.

Seine and Piave are silver spoons,
But the spoonbowl-metal is thin and worn,
There are English counties like hunting-tunes
Played on the keys of a postboy's horn,
But I will remember where I was born.

I will remember Carquinez Straits,
Little French Lick and Lundy's Lane,
The Yankee ships and the Yankee dates
And the bullet-towns of Calamity Jane.
I will remember Skunktown Plain.

I will fall in love with a Salem tree
And a rawhide quirt from Santa Cruz,
I will get me a bottle of Boston sea
And a blue-gum nigger to sing me blues.
I am tired of loving a foreign muse.

Rue des Martyrs and Bleeding-Heart-Yard,
Senlis, Pisa and Blindman's Oast,
It is a magic ghost you guard;
But I am sick for a newer ghost—
Harrisburg, Spartanburg, Painted Post.

Henry and John were never so,
And Henry and John were always right?
Granted, but when it was time to go
And the tea and the laurels had stood all night,
Did they never watch for Nantucket Light?

I shall not rest quiet in Montparnasse.
I shall not lie easy in Winchelsea.
You may bury my body in Sussex grass,
You may bury my tongue at Champmédy.
I shall not be there. I shall rise and pass.
Bury my heart at Wounded Knee.

The Fourth of July

JOHN PIERPONT
(1785–1866)

Day of glory! Welcome day!
Freedom's banners greet thy ray;
See! how cheerfully they play
    With thy morning breeze,
On the rocks where pilgrims kneeled,
On the heights where squadrons wheeled,
When a tyrant's thunder pealed
    O'er the trembling seas.

God of armies! did thy stars
On their courses smite his cars;
Blast his arm, and wrest his bars
    From the heaving tide?
On our standard, lo! they burn,
And, when days like this return,
Sparkle o'er the soldier's urn
    Who for freedom died.

God of peace! whose spirit fills
All the echoes of our hills,
All the murmur of our rills,
    Now the storm is o'er,
O let freemen be our sons,
And let future Washingtons
Rise, to lead their valiant ones
    Til there's war no more!

Boston Hymn
Read in Boston Music Hall,
January 1, 1863
RALPH WALDO EMERSON
(1803–1882)

The word of the Lord by night
To the watching Pilgrims came,
As they sat by the seaside,
And filled their hearts with flame.

God said, I am tired of kings,
I suffer them no more;
Up to my ear the morning brings
The outrage of the poor.

Think ye I made this ball
A field of havoc and war,
Where tyrants great and tyrants small
Might harry the weak and poor?

My angel, his name is Freedom—
Choose him to be your king;
She shall cut pathways east and west,
And fend you with his wing.

Lo! I uncover the land
Which I hid of old time in the West,
As the sculptor uncovers the statue
When he has wrought his best;

I show Columbia, of the rocks
Which dip their foot in the seas,
And soar to the airborne flocks
Of clouds, and the boreal fleece.

I will divide my goods;
Call in the wretch and slave:
None shall rule but the humble.
And none but toil shall have.

I will have never a noble,
No lineage counted great;
Fishers and choppers and ploughmen
Shall constitute a state.

Go, cut down trees in the forest.
And trim the straightest boughs;
Cut down the trees in the forest,
And build me a wooded house.

Call the people together,
The young men and the sires,
The digger in the harvest field,
Hireling, and him that hires;

And here in a pine statehouse
They shall choose men to rule
In every needful faculty,
In church, and state, and school.

Lo, now! if these poor men
Can govern the land and sea,
And make just laws below the sun,
As planets faithful be.

And ye shall succor men;
'Tis nobleness to serve;
Help them who cannot help again:
Beware from right to swerve.

I break your bonds and masterships,
And I unchain the slave:

Free be his heart and hand henceforth
As wind and wandering wave.

I cause from every creature
His proper good to flow:
As much as he is and doeth,
So much he shall bestow.

But laying hands on another
To coin his labor and sweat,
He goes in pawn to his victim
For eternal years in debt.

Today unbind the captive
So only are ye unbound;
Lift up a people from the dust,
Trump of their rescue, sound!

Pay ransom to the owner,
And fill the bag to the brim.
Who is the owner? The slave is owner,
And ever was. Pay him.

Oh North! give him beauty for rags,
And honor. O South! for his shame;
Nevada! coin thy golden crags
With Freedom's image and name.

Up! And the dusky race
That sat in darness long—
Be swift their feet as antelopes,
And as behemoth strong.

Come, East and West and North.
By races, as snowflakes,
And carry my purpose forth,
Which neither halts nor shakes.

My will fulfilled shall be,
For, in daylight or in dark,
My thunderbolt has eyes to see
His way home to the mark.

America Befriend

HENRY VAN DYKE

(1852–1933)

O Lord, our God, Thy mighty hand
   Hath made our country free;
From all her broad and happy land
   May worship rise to Thee.
Fulfill the promise of her youth,
   Her liberty defend;
By law and order, love and truth,
   America befriend!

The strength of every state increase
   In Union's golden chain;
Her thousand cities fill with peace,
   Her million fields with grain:
The virtues of her mingled blood
   In one new people blend;
By unity and brotherhood,
   America befriend!

O suffer not her feet to stray;
   But guide her untaught might,
That she may walk in peaceful day,
   And lead the world in light.
Bring down the proud, lift up the poor,
   Unequal ways amend;
By justice, nation-wide and sure,
   America befriend!

Through all the waiting land proclaim
   The gospel of good-will;
And may the joy of Jesus' name
   In every bosom thrill.
O'er hill and vale, from sea to sea,
   Thy holy reign extend;
By faith and hope and charity,
   America befriend!

Columbia

TIMOTHY DWIGHT

(1758–1817)

Columbia, Columbia, to glory arise,
The queen of the world, and the child of the skies;
Thy genius commands thee; with rapture behold,
While ages on ages thy splendor unfold,
Thy reign is the last, and the noblest of time,
Most fruitful thy soil, most inviting thy clime;
Let the crimes of the east ne'er encrimson thy name,
Be freedom, and science, and virtue thy fame.

To conquest and slaughter let Europe aspire:
Whelm nations in blood, and wrap cities in fire;
Thy heroes the rights of mankind shall defend,
And triumph pursue them, and glory attend.
A world is thy realm: for a world be thy laws,
Enlarge as thine empire, and just as thy cause;
On Freedom's broad basis, that empire shall rise,
Extend with the main, and dissolve with the skies.

Fair Science her gates to thy sons shall unbar,
And the east see the morn hide the beams of her star.
New bards, and new sages, unrivaled shall soar
To fame unextinguished, when time is no more;
To thee, the last refuge of virtue designed,
Shall fly from all nations the best of mankind;
Here, grateful to Heaven, with transport shall bring
Their incense, more fragrant than odors of spring. . . .

Thy fleets to all regions thy power shall display,
The nations admire and the ocean obey;
Each shore to thy glory its tribute unfold,
And the east and the south yield their spices and gold.
As the day-spring unbounded, thy splendor shall flow,
And earth's little kingdoms before thee shall bow;
While the ensigns of union, in triumph unfurled,
Hush the tumult of war and give peace to the world.

Thus, as down a lone valley, with cedars o'er-spread,
From war's dread confusion I pensively strayed,
The gloom from the face of fair heaven retired;
Perfumes as of Eden flowed sweetly along,
And a voice as of angels, enchantingly sung:
"Columbia, Columbia, to glory arise,
The queen of the world, and the child of the skies."

Battle Hymn of the Republic

JULIA WARD HOWE

(1819–1910)

Mine eyes have seen the glory of the coming of the
    Lord:
He is trampling out the vintage where the grapes of
    wrath are stored;
He hath loosed the fateful lightning of his terrible
    swift sword:
        His truth is marching on.

I have seen Him in the watch-fires of a hundred
    circling camps;
They have builded Him an altar in the evening dews
    and damps;
I can read his righteous sentence by the dim and
    flaring lamps.
        His day is marching on.

I have read a fiery gospel, writ in burnished rows of
    steel:
"As ye deal with my contemners, so with you my grace
    shall deal;
Let the Hero, born of woman, crush the serpent with
    his heel,
        Since God is marching on."

He has sounded forth the trumpet that shall never call
    retreat;
He is sifting out the hearts of men before his
    judgment-seat:
Oh! be swift, my soul, to answer Him! be jubilant, my
    feet!
        Our God is marching on.

In the beauty of the lilies Christ was born across the
    sea,

With a glory in his bosom that transfigures you and
me:
As He died to make men holy, let us die to make men
free,
While God is marching on.

Oath of Allegiance

I pledge allegiance to the Flag of the United States of
America and to the Republic for which it stands—one
Nation indivisible with Liberty and Justice for all.

The Flag Goes By

HENRY HOLCOMB BENNETT
(1863–1924)

Hats off!
Along the street there comes
A blare of bugles, a ruffle of drums,
A flash of color beneath the sky:
Hats off!
The flag is passing by!

Blue and crimson and white it shines,
Over the steel-tipped, ordered lines.
Hats off!
The colors before us fly;
But more than the flag is passing by.

Sea-flights and land-fights, grim and great,
Fought to make and to save the State:
Weary marches and sinking ships;
Cheers of victory on dying lips;

Days of plenty and years of peace;
March of a strong land's swift increase;
Equal justice, right and law,
Stately honor and reverend awe;

Sign of a nation, great and strong
To ward her people from foreign wrong:
Pride and glory and honor,—all
Live in the colors to stand or fall.

Hats off!
Along the street there comes
A blare of bugles, a ruffle of drums;
And loyal hearts are beating high:
Hats off!
The flag is passing by!

America

SAMUEL FRANCIS SMITH
(1808–1895)

My country, 'tis of thee,
Sweet land of liberty,
    Of thee I sing;
Land where my fathers died,
Land of the pilgrims' pride,
From every mountain-side
    Let freedom ring.

My native country, thee,
Land of the noble free,
    Thy name I love;
I love thy rocks and rills,
Thy woods and templed hills;
My heart with rapture thrills
    Like that above.

Let music swell the breeze,
And ring from all the trees
    Sweet freedom's song;
Let mortal tongues awake,
Let all that breathe partake,
Let rocks their silence break—
    The sound prolong.

Our fathers' God, to Thee,
Author of liberty,
    To Thee we sing;
Long may our land be bright
With freedom's holy light;
Protect us by Thy might,
    Great God, our King.

A National Hymn

From *Miss Ravenel's Conversion*

JOHN WILLIAM DEFOREST

(1826–1906)

Be thou our country's Chief
In this our age of grief,
   Allfather great;
Go forth with awful tread,
Crush treason's serpent head,
Bring back our sons misled,
   And save our State.

Uphold our stripes and stars
Through war's destroying jars
   With thy right hand;
O God of battles, lead
Where our swift navies speed,
Where our brave armies bleed
   For fatherland.

Break every yoke and chain,
Let truth and justice reign
   From sea to sea;
Make all our statutes right
In thy most holy sight;
Light us, O Lord of light,
   To follow Thee.

God bless our fatherland,
God make it strong and grand
   On sea and shore;
Ages its glory swell,
Peace in its borders dwell,
God stand its sentinel
   For evermore.

The Gift Outright

Robert Frost
(1874–1963)

The land was ours before we were the land's.
She was our land more than a hundred years
Before we were her people. She was ours
In Massachusetts, in Virginia,
But we were England's, still colonials,
Possessing what we still were unpossessed by,
Possessed by what we now no more possessed.
Something we were withholding made us weak
Until we found out that it was ourselves
We were withholding from our land of living,
And forthwith found salvation in surrender.
Such as we were we gave ourselves outright
(The deed of gift was many deeds of war)
To the land vaguely realizing westward,
But still unstoried, artless, unenhanced,
Such as she was, such as she would become.

Lift Every Voice and Sing

JAMES W. JOHNSON

(1871-1938)

Lift every voice and sing
Till earth and heaven ring,
Ring with the harmonies of liberty.
Let our rejoicing rise
High as the list'ning skies;
Let it resound loud as the rolling sea.
Sing a song full of the faith that the dark past has
  taught us;
Sing a song full of the hope that the present has
  brought us;
Facing the rising sun
Of our new day begun,
Let us march on, till victory is won.

Stony the road we trod,
Bitter the chast'ning rod,
Felt in the days when hope unborn had died;
Yet, with a steady beat,
Have not our weary feet
Come to the place for which our parents sighed?
We have come over a way that with tears has been
  watered;
We have come, treading our path through the blood of
  the slaughtered,
Out from the gloomy past,
Till now we stand at last
Where the white gleam of our bright star is cast.

God of our weary years,
God of our silent tears,
Thou who hast brought us thus far on the way;
Thou who hast by thy might
Led us into the light:
Keep us forever in the path, we pray.
Lest our feet stray from the places, our God, where we
  met thee;

Lest, our hearts drunk with the wine of the world, we
    forget thee;
Shadowed beneath thy hand
May we forever stand,
True to our God, true to our native land.

Concord Hymn
Sung at the completion of the Battle
Monument, April 19, 1886
RALPH WALDO EMERSON
(1803–1882)

By the rude bridge that arched the flood,
    Their flag to April's breeze unfurled,
Here once the embattled farmers stood,
    And fired the shot heard round the world.

The foe long since in silence slept;
    Alike the conqueror silent sleeps;
And Time the ruined bridge has swept
    Down the dark stream which seaward creeps.

On the green bank, by this soft stream,
    We set today a votive stone;
That memory may their deed redeem,
    When, like our sires, our sons are gone.

Spirit, that made those spirits dare
    To die, and leave their children free,
Bid Time and Nature gently spare
    The shaft we raise to them and thee.

Breathes There the Man

From *"The Lay of the Last Minstrel,"*
CANTO VI.

SIR WALTER SCOTT
(1771-1832)

Breathes there the man with soul so dead
Who never to himself hath said,
  This is my own, my native land!
Whose heart hath ne'er within him burned,
As home his footsteps he hath turned
  From wandering on a foreign strand?
If such there breathe, go, mark him well;
For him no minstrel raptures swell;
High though his titles, proud his name,
Boundless his wealth as wish can claim,
Despite those titles, power, and pelf,
The wretch, concentred all in self,
Living, shall forfeit fair renown,
And, doubly dying, shall go down
To the vile dust from whence he sprung,
Unwept, unhonored, and unsung.

I Am an American

ELIAS LIEBERMAN
(1883–?)

"I am an American.
My father belongs to the Sons of the Revolution.
My mother to the Colonial Dames.
One of my ancestors pitched tea overboard in Boston
    Harbor,
Another stood his ground with Warren,
Another hungered with Washington at Valley Forge.
My ancestors were Americans in the making.
They spoke in her council-halls,
They died on her battle-ships,
They cleared her forests.
Dawn reddened and paled.
Stanch hearts of mine beat fast at each new star
In the nation's flag.
Keen eyes of mine foresaw her greater glory—
The sweep of her seas,
The plenty of her plains,
The man-hives of her billion-wired cities.
Every drop of blood in me holds a heritage of
    patriotism.
I am an American!"

Then the Russian Jew speaks—
"I am an American.
My father was an atom of dust,
My mother a straw in the wind,
To His Serene Majesty.
One of my ancestors died in the mines of Siberia,
Another was crippled for life by twenty blows of the
    knout,
Another was killed defending his home during the
    massacres.
The history of my ancestors is a trail of blood

To the palace gates of the Great White Czar.
But then the dream came—
The dream of America.
In the light of the Liberty torch
The atom of dust became a man,
And the straw in the wind became a woman,
For the first time.

'See,' said my father, pointing to the flag that fluttered
    near,
'That flag of stars and stripes is yours.
It is the emblem of the Promised Land.
It means, my son, the hope of humanity.
Live for it, die for it.'
Under the open sky of my new country
I swore to do so,
And every drop of blood in me
Will keep that vow.
I am proud of my future.
I am an American!

God Save the Flag

OLIVER WENDELL HOLMES
(1809–1894)

Washed in the blood of the brave and the blooming,
   Snatched from the altars of insolent foes,
Burning with star-fires, but never consuming,
   Flash its broad ribbons of lily and rose.

Vainly the prophets of Baal would rend it,
   Vainly his worshippers pray for its fall;
Thousands have died for it, millions defend it,
   Emblem of justice and mercy to all:

Justice that reddens the sky with her terrors,
   Mercy that comes with her white-handed train,
Soothing all passions, redeeming all errors,
   Sheathing the sabre and breaking the chain.

Borne on the deluge of old usurpations,
   Drifted our Ark o'er the desolate seas,
Bearing the rainbow of hope to the nations,
   Torn from the storm-cloud and flung to the breeze!

God bless the Flag and its loyal defenders,
   While its broad folds o'er the battle-field wave,
Till the dim star-wealth rekindle its splendors,
   Washed from its strains in the blood of the brave!

A Nation's Strength

RALPH WALDO EMERSON

(1803–1882)

What makes a nation's pillars high
  And its foundations strong?
What makes it mighty to defy
  The foes that round it throng?

It is not gold. Its kingdoms grand
  Go down in battle shock;
Its shafts are laid on sinking sand,
  Not on abiding rock.

Is it the sword? Ask the red dust
  Of empires passed away;
The blood has turned their stones to rust,
  Their glory to decay.

And is it pride? Ah, that bright crown
  Has seemed to nations sweet;
But God has struck its luster down
  In ashes at his feet.

Not gold but only men can make
  A people great and strong;
Men who for truth and honor's sake
  Stand fast and suffer long.

Brave men who work while others sleep,
  Who dare while others fly—
They build a nation's pillars deep
  And lift them to the sky.

Not Alone for Mighty Empire

WILLIAM PIERSON MERRILL
(1867–1954)

Not alone for mighty empire,
Stretching far o'er land and sea;
Not alone for bounteous harvests,
Lift we up our hearts to Thee.
Standing in the living present,
Memory and hope between,
Lord, we would with deep thanksgiving
Praise Thee most for things unseen.

Not for battleship and fortress,
Not for conquests of the sword
But for conquests of the spirit
Give we thanks to Thee, O Lord;
For the priceless gift of freedom,
For the home, the church, the school;
For the open door to manhood
In a land the people rule.

For the armies of the faithful,
Souls that passed and left no name;
For the glory that illumines
Patriot lives of deathless fame;
For our prophets and apostles,
Loyal to the living Word;
For all heroes of the Spirit
Give we thanks to Thee, O Lord.

God of justice, save the people
From the clash of race and creed,
From the strife of class and faction;
Make our nation free indeed.
Keep her faith in simple manhood
Strong as when her life began,
Till it finds its full fruition
In the brotherhood of man.

Pioneers! O Pioneers!

WALT WHITMAN
(1819–1892)

Come my tan-faced children,
Follow well in order, get your weapons ready,
Have you your pistols? have you your sharp-edged
axes?
Pioneers! O pioneers!

For we cannot tarry here,
We must march my darlings, we must bear the brunt
of danger,
We the youthful sinewy races, all the rest on us
depend,
Pioneers! O pioneers!

O you youths, Western youths,
So impatient, full of action, full of manly pride and
friendship,
Plain I see you Western youths, see you tramping with
the foremost,
Pioneers! O pioneers!

Have the elder races halted?
Do they droop and end their lesson, wearied over there
beyond the seas
We take up the task eternal, and the burden and the
lesson,
Pioneers! O pioneers!

All the past we leave behind,
We debouch upon a newer mightier world, varied
world,
Fresh and strong the world we seize, world of labor
and the march,
Pioneers! O pioneers!

We detachments steady throwing,
Down the edges, through the passes, up the mountains
steep,

Conquering, holding, daring, venturing as we go the
        unknown ways,
                Pioneers! O pioneers!

                We primeval forests felling,
We the rivers stemming, vexing we and piercing deep
        the mind within,
We the surface broad surveying, we the virgin soil
        upheaving,
                Pioneers! O pioneers!

                Colorado men are we,
From the peaks gigantic, from the great sierras and
        the high plateaus,
From the mine and from the gully, from the hunting
        trail we come,
                Pioneers! O pioneers!

                From Nebraska, from Arkansas,
Central inland race are we, from Missouri, with the
        continental blood intervein'd,
All the hands of comrades clasping, all the Southern,
        all the Northern,
                Pioneers! O pioneers!

                O resistless restless race!
O beloved race in all! O my breast aches with tender
        love for all,
O I mourn and yet exult, I am rapt with love for all,
                Pioneers! O pioneers!

                Raise the mighty mother mistress,
Waving high the delicate mistress, over all the starry
        mistress (bend your heads all,)
Raise the fang'd and warlike mistress, stern,
        impassive, weapon'd mistress,
                Pioneers! O pioneers!

                See my children, resolute
                children,
By those swarms upon our rear we must never yield or
        falter,

Ages back in ghostly millions frowning there behind
us urging,
Pioneers! O pioneers!

On and on the compact ranks,
With accessions ever waiting, with the places of the
dead quickly fill'd,
Through the battle, through defeat, moving yet and
never stopping,
Pioneers! O pioneers!

O to die advancing on!
Are there some of us to droop and die? has the hour
come?
Then upon the march we fittest die, soon and sure the
gap is fill'd,
Pioneers! O pioneers!

All the pulses of the world,
Falling in they beat for us, with the Western
movement beat,
Holding single or together, steady moving to the front,
all for us,
Pioneers! O pioneers!

Life's involv'd and varied
pageants,
All the forms and shows, all the workmen at their
work,
All the seamen and the landsmen, all the masters with
their slaves,
Pioneers! O pioneers!

All the hapless silent lovers,
All the prisoners in the prisons, all the righteous and
the wicked,
All the joyous, all the sorrowing, all the living, all the
dying,
Pioneers! O pioneers!

56

I too with my soul and body,
We, a curious trio, picking, wandering on our way,
Through these shores amid the shadows, with the
apparitions pressing,
Pioneers! O pioneers!

Lo, the darting bowling orb!
Lo, the brother orbs around, all the clustering suns
and planets,
All the dazzling days, all the mystic nights with
dreams,
Pioneers! O pioneers!

These are of us, they are with us,
All for primal needed work, while the followers there
in embryo wait behind,
We to-day's procession heading, we the route for travel
clearing
Pioneers! O pioneers!

O you daughters of the West!
O you young and elder daughters! O you mothers and
you wives!
Never must you be divided, in our ranks you move
united,
Pioneers! O pioneers!

Minstrels latent on the prairies!
(Shrouded bards of other lands, you may rest, you have
done your work,)
Soon I hear you coming warbling, soon you rise and
tramp amid us,
Pioneers! O pioneers:

Not for delectations sweet,
Not the cushion and the slipper, not the peaceful and
the studious,
Not the riches safe and palling, not for us the tame
enjoyment,
Pioneers! O pioneers!

Do the feasters gluttonous feast?
Do the corpulent sleepers sleep? have they lock'd and
bolted doors?
Still be ours the diet hard, and the blanket on the
ground,
Pioneers! O pioneers!

Has the night descended?
Was the road of late so toilsome? did we stop
discouraged nodding on our way?
Yet a passing hour I yield you in your tracks to pause
oblivious,
Pioneers! O pioneers!

Till with sound of trumpet,
Far, far off the daybreak call—hark! how loud and
clear I hear it wind,
Swift! to the head of the army!—swift! spring to your
places,
Pioneers! O pioneers!

The Poor Voter on Election Day

JOHN GREENLEAF WHITTIER
(1807–1892)

The proudest now is but my peer,
  The highest not more high;
Today, of all the weary year,
  A king of men am I.
Today, alike are great and small,
  The nameless and the known;
My palace is the people's hall,
  The ballot-box my throne!

Who serves today upon the list
  Beside the served shall stand;
Alike the brown and wrinkled fist,
  The gloved and dainty hand!
The rich is level with the poor,
  The weak is strong today;
And sleekest broadcloth counts no more
  Than homespun frock of gray.

Today let pomp and vain pretense
  My stubborn right abide;
I set a plain man's common sense
  Against the pedant's pride.
Today shall simple manhood try
  The strength of gold and land;
The wide world has not wealth to buy
  The power in my right hand!

While there's a grief to seek redress,
  Or balance to adjust,
Where weighs our living manhood less
  Than Mammon's vilest dust—
While there's a right to need my vote,
  A wrong to sweep away,
Up! clouted knee and ragged coat!
  A man's a man today!

Oh Mother of a Mighty Race

William Cullen Bryant
(1794–1878)

Oh mother of a mighty race,
Yet lovely in thy youthful grace!
The elder dames, thy haughty peers,
Admire and hate thy blooming years.
   With words of shame
And taunts of scorn they join thy name.

For on thy cheeks the glow is spread
That tints thy morning hills with red;
Thy step—the wild deer's rustling feet
Within thy woods are not more fleet;
   Thy hopeful eye
Is bright as thine own sunny sky.

Ay, let them rail—those haughty ones,
While safe thou dwellest with thy sons.
They do not know how loved thou art,
How many a fond and fearless heart
   Would rise to throw
Its life between thee and the foe.

They know not, in their hate and pride,
What virtues with thy children bide;
How true, how good, thy graceful maids
Make bright, like flowers, the valley-shades;
   What generous men
Spring, like thine oaks, by hill and glen;—

What cordial welcomes greet the guest
By thy lone rivers of the West.
How faith is kept, and truth revered,
And man is loved, and God is feared,
   In woodland homes,
And where the ocean border foams.

There's freedom at thy gates and rest
For Earth's downtrodden and oppressed,
A shelter for the hunted head.
For the starved laborer toil and bread.
   Power, at thy bounds,
Stops and calls back his baffled hounds.

Oh, fair young mother! on thy brow
Shall sit a nobler grace than now.
Deep in the brightness of the skies
The thronging years in glory rise.
   And, as they fleet,
Drop strength and riches at thy feet.

The People's Prayer
AMOS R. WELLS
(1862–1933)

God bless our dear United States,
Preserve the land from evil fates,
Lift high her banner fair and free,
And guard her bounds from sea to sea.

From foe without and foe within,
From open shame and hidden sin,
From boastful pride and greedy store,
God keep our nation evermore.

Forever may her friendly hands
Receive the poor of other lands
In kindliness of sisterhood,
And fill their arms with ample good.

Assailed by battle hosts of wrong,
God help our country to be strong.
Assailed by falsehood's crafty crew,
God help our country to be true.

God hold the nation's aim sincere,
God save her heart from coward fear.
God prosper her in true success,
And crown her head with worthiness.

God bless our dear United States,
Preserve the land from evil fates,
Lift high her banner fair and free,
And ever guard her liberty.

Columbia, the Gem
of the Ocean

First sung in Philadelphia about 1843

AUTHOR UNKNOWN

O Columbia, the gem of the ocean,
  The home of the brave and the free,
The shrine of each patriot's devotion,
  A world offers homage to thee.
Thy mandates make heroes assemble
  When Liberty's form stands in view;
Thy banners make tyranny tremble
  When borne by the red, white and blue.
    When borne by the red, white and blue,
    When borne by the red, white and blue,
    Thy banners make tyranny tremble
    When borne by the red, white and blue.

When war winged its wide desolation
    And threatened the land to deform,
The ark then of freedom's foundation,
    Columbia, rode safe thro' the storm:
With the garlands of vict'ry around her,
    When so proudly she bore her brave crew,
With her flag proudly floating before her,
    The boast of the red, white and blue,
        The boast of the red, white and blue,
        The boast of the red, white and blue,
        With her flag proudly floating before her,
        The boast of the red, white and blue.

The star-spangled banner bring hither,
    O'er Columbia's true sons let it wave;
May the wreaths they have won never wither,
    Nor its stars cease to shine on the brace:
May the service, united, ne'er sever,
    But hold to their colors so true;
The army and navy forever,
    Three cheers for the red, white and blue.
        Three cheers for the red, white and blue,
        Three cheers for the red, white and blue,
        The army and navy forever.
        Three cheers for the red, white and blue.

The Star-Spangled Banner

FRANCIS SCOTT KEY

(1779–1843)

O say, can you see, by the dawn's early light,
  What so proudly we hailed at the twilight's last
    gleaming?
Whose broad stripes and bright stars, through the
    perilous fight,
  O'er the ramparts we watched were so gallantly
    streaming!
And the rocket's red glare, the bombs bursting in air,
Gave proof through the night that our flag was still
    there:
  O say, does that star-spangled banner yet wave
  O'er the land of the free and the home of the brave?

On the shore, dimly seen through the mists of the deep,
  Where the foe's haughty host in dread silence
    reposes,
What is that which the breeze, o'er the towering steep,
  As it fitfully blows, now conceals, now discloses?
Now it catches the gleam of the morning's first beam,
In full glory reflected now shines on the stream:
  'Tis the star-spangled banner! O long may it wave
  O'er the land of the free and the home of the brave!

And where is that band who so vauntingly swore
  That the havoc of war and the battle's confusion
A home and a country should leave us no more?
  Their blood has washed out their foul footsteps'
    pollution.
No refuge could save the hireling and slave
From the terror of flight, or the gloom of the grave:
  And the star-spangled banner in triumph doth wave
  O'er the land of the free and the home of the brave!

Oh! thus be it ever, when freemen shall stand
  Between their loved homes and the war's desolation!
Blest with victory and peace, may the heaven-rescued
    land

Praise the Power that hath made and preserved us a
    nation.
Then conquer we must, for our cause it is just,
And this be our motto: "In God is our trust."
    And the star-spangled banner in triumph shall wave
O'er the land of the free and the home of the brave.

The Republic
From "The Building of the Ship"

HENRY WADSWORTH LONGFELLOW
(1807–1882)

Thou, too, sail on, O Ship of State!
Sail on, O Union, strong and great!
Humanity with all its fears,
With all the hopes of future years,
Is hanging breathless on thy fate!
We know what Master laid thy keel,
What Workmen wrought thy ribs of steel,
Who made each mast, and sail, and rope,
What anvils rang, what hammers beat,
In what a forge and what a heat
Were shaped the anchors of thy hope!
Fear not each sudden sound and shock,
'Tis of the wave and not the rock;
'Tis but the flapping of the sail,
And not a rent made by the gale!
In spite of rock and tempest's roar,
In spite of false lights on the shore,
Sail on, nor fear to breast the sea!
Our heart, our hopes, are all with thee,
Our hearts, our hopes, our prayers, our tears,
Our faith triumphant o'er our fears,
Are all with thee—are all with thee!

The Flower of Liberty
OLIVER WENDELL HOLMES
(1809–1894)

What flower is this that greets the morn,
Its hues from Heaven so freshly born?
With burning star and flaming band
It kindles all the sunset land:
Oh tell us what the name may be—
Is this the Flower of Liberty?
  It is the banner of the free,
   The starry Flower of Liberty!

In savage Nature's far abode
Its tender seed our fathers sowed;
The storm-winds rocked its swelling bud,
Its opening leaves were streaked with blood,
Till lo! earth's tyrants shook to see
The full-blown Flower of Liberty!
  Then hail the banner of the free,
   The starry Flower of Liberty!

Behold its streaming rays unite,
One mingling flood of braided light—
The red that fires the Southern rose,
With spotless white from Northern snows,
And, spangled o'er its azure, see
The sister Stars of Liberty!
  Then hail the banner of the free,
   The starry Flower of Liberty!

The blades of heroes fence it round,
Where'er it springs is holy ground;
From tower and dome its glories spread;
It waves where lonely sentries tread;
It makes the land as ocean free,
And plants an empire on the sea!
  Then hail the banner of the free,
  The starry Flower of Liberty!

Thy sacred leaves, fair Freedom's flower,
Shall ever float on dome and tower,
To all their heavenly colors true,
In blackening frost or crimson dew,—
And God love us as we love thee,
Thrice holy Flower of Liberty!
  Then hail the banner of the free,
  The starry Flower of Liberty!

The Blue and the Gray

FRANCIS MILES FINCH
(1827–1907)

By the flow of the inland river,
  Whence the fleets of iron have fled,
Where the blades of the grave grass quiver,
  Asleep are the ranks of the dead;—
    Under the sod and the dew,
      Waiting the judgment day;—
    Under the one, the Blue;
      Under the other, the Gray.

These in the robings of glory,
  Those in the gloom of defeat,
All with the battle blood gory,
  In the dusk of eternity meet;—
    Under the sod and the dew,
      Waiting the judgment day;—
    Under the laurel, the Blue;
      Under the willow, the Gray.

From the silence of sorrowful hours
  The desolate mourners go,
Lovingly laden with flowers
  Alike for the friend and the foe,—
    Under the sod and the dew,
      Waiting the judgment day;—
    Under the roses, the Blue;
      Under the lilies, the Gray.

So with an equal splendor
  The morning sun rays fall,
With a touch, impartially tender,
  On the blossoms blooming for all,—
    Under the sod and the dew,
      Waiting the judgment day;—
    'Broidered with gold, the Blue;
      Mellowed with gold, the Gray.

So, when the summer calleth,
  On forest and field of grain
With an equal murmur falleth
  The cooling drip of the rain;—
    Under the sod and the dew,
      Waiting the judgment day;—
    Wet with the rain, the Blue;
      Wet with the rain, the Gray.

Sadly, but not with upbraiding,
  The generous deed was done;
In the storm of the years that are fading,
  No braver battle was won;—
    Under the sod and the dew,
      Waiting the judgment day;—
    Under the blossoms, the Blue;
      Under the garlands, the Gray.

No more shall the war cry sever,
  Or the winding rivers be red;
They banish our anger forever
  When they laurel the graves of our dead!
    Under the sod and the dew,
      Waiting the judgment day;—
    Love and tears for the Blue,
      Tears and love for the Gray.

Lines on the Back of a Confederate Note

Maj. Samuel Alroy Jonas

Representing nothing on God's earth now,
    And naught in the waters below it,
As the pledge of a nation that's dead and gone,
    Keep it, dear friends, and show it.

Show it to those who will lend an ear
    To the tale that this trifle can tell,
Of a liberty born of a patriot's dream,
    Of a storm-cradled nation that fell.

Too poor to possess the precious ores,
    And too much of a stranger to borrow,
We issued today our promise to pay
    And hoped to redeem on the morrow.

The days rolled by and the weeks became years,
    But our coffers were empty still.
Coin was so rare that the treasury'd quake
    If a dollar dropped into the till.

But the faith that was in us was strong indeed,
    And our poverty well we discerned,
And this little note represented the pay
    That our suffering veterans earned.

They knew it had hardly a value in gold,
    Yet as gold each soldier received it.
It gazed in our eyes with a promise to pay,
    And every true soldier believed it.

But our boys thought little of price or of pay,
    Or of bills that were long past due;
We knew if it brought us our bread today,
    'Twas the best our poor country could do.
Keep it; it tells all our history over,
    From the birth of the dream to its last:
Modest and born of the Angel of Hope,
    Like our hope of success it has passed.

The Land Where Hate Should Die

DENIS A. MCCARTHY

(1870–1931)

This is the land where hate should die—
　No feuds of faith, no spleen of race,
No darkly brooding fear should try
　Beneath our flag to find a place.
Lo! every people here has sent
　Its sons to answer freedom's call;
Their lifeblood is the strong cement
　That builds and binds the nation's wall.

This is the land where hate should die—
　Though dear to me my faith and shrine,
I serve my country well when I
　Respect beliefs that are not mine.
He little loves his land who'd cast
　Upon his neighbor's word a doubt,
Or cite the wrongs of ages past
　From present rights to bar him out.

This is the land where hate should die—
　This is the land where strife should cease,
Where foul, suspicious fear should fly
　Before our flag of light and peace.
Then let us purge from poisoned thought
　That service to the state we give,
And so be worthy as we ought
　Of this great land in which we live!

I Am the Flag

LAWRENCE M. JONES

I am a composite being of all the people of America.
I am the union if you are united.
I am one and indivisible if you are undivided.
I am as strong as the weakest link.
I am an emblem of your country.
I am a symbol of a shadow of the real.
I am a sign pointing to past achievements.
I am a promise of greater things for the future.
I am what you make me.
I am purity if you are pure.
I am bravery if you are brave.
I am loyalty if you are loyal.

I am honor if you are honorable.
I am goodness if you are good.
I am hope if you are hopeful.
I am truth if you are true.

I am the Constitution.
I am law and order.
I am tolerance or intolerance as you force me to be.
I am liberty as you understand liberty.
I am as a pillar of fire by night, but you must provide
    the fuel.

I march at the head of the column, but you must carry
    me on.

I stand for greater and more glorious achievement
    than can be found in recorded history, but you
    must be my inspiration.

I AM THE FLAG.

One Country

FRANK L. STANTON

(1857-1927)

After all,
One country, brethren! We must rise or fall
With the Supreme Republic. We must be
The makers of her immortality;
  Her freedom, fame,
  Her glory or her shame—
Liegemen to God and fathers of the free!

After all—
Hark! from the heights the clear, strong, clarion call
And the command imperious: "Stand forth,
Sons of the South and brothers of the North!
  Stand forth and be
  As one one soil and sea—
Your country's honor more than empire's worth!"

After all,
'Tis Freedom wears the loveliest coronal;
Her brow is to the morning; in the sod
She breathes the breath of patriots; every clod
  Answers her call
  And rises like a wall
Against the foes of liberty and God!

Our Country

Julia Ward Howe
(1819–1910)

On primal rocks she wrote her name;
  Her towers were reared on holy graves;
The golden seed that bore her came
  Swift-winged with prayer on ocean waves.

The Forest bowed his solemn crest,
  And open flung his sylvan doors;
Meek Rivers led the appointed guest
  To clasp the wide-embracing shores;

Till, fold by fold, the broidered land
  To swell her virgin vestments grew,
While sages, strong in heart and hand,
  Her virtue's fiery girdle drew.

O exile of the wrath of kings!
  O Pilgrim Ark of Liberty!
The refuge of divinest things,
  Their record must abide in thee!

First in the glories of thy front
  Let the crown-jewel, Truth, be found;
Thy right hand fling, with generous wont,
  Love's happy chain to farthest bound!

Let Justice, with the faultless scales,
  Hold fast the worship of thy sons;
Thy Commerce spread her shining sails
  Where no dark tide of rapine runs!

So link thy ways to those of God,
  So follow firm the heavenly laws,
That stars may greet thee, warrior-browed,
  And storm-sped angels hail thy cause!

O Lord, the measure of our prayers,
  Hope of the world in grief and wrong,
Be thine the tribute of the years,
  The gift of Faith, the crown of Song!

Centennial Hymn

John Greenleaf Whittier
(1808–1892)

I

Our fathers' God! from out whose hand
The centuries fall like grains of sand,
We meet to-day, united, free,
And loyal to our land and Thee,
To thank Thee for the era done,
And trust Thee for the opening one.

II

Here, where of old, by Thy design,
The fathers spake that word of Thine
Whose echo is the glad refrain
Of rended bolt and falling chain,
To grace our festal time, from all
The zones of earth our guest we call.

III

Be with us while the New World greets
The Old World thronging all its streets,
Unveiling all the triumphs won
By art or toil beneath the sun;
And unto common good ordain
This rivalship of hand and brain.

IV

Thou, who hast here in concord furled
The war flags of a gathered world,
Beneath our Western skies fulfil
The Orient's mission of good-will,
And, freighted with love's Golden Fleece,
Send back its Argonauts of peace.

V

For art and labor met in truce,
For beauty made the bride of use,
We thank Thee; but, withal, we crave
The austere virtues strong to save,
The honor proof to place or gold,
The manhood never bought nor sold!

VI

Oh make Thou us, through centuries long,
In peace secure, in justice strong;
Around our gift of freedom draw
The safeguards of Thy righteous law:
And, cast in some diviner mould,
Let the new cycle shame the old!

For You O Democracy

Walt Whitman
(1819–1892)

Come, I will make the continent indissoluble,
I will make the most splendid race the sun ever shone
    upon,
I will make divine magnetic lands,
    With the love of comrades,
       With the life-long love of comrades.

I will plant companionship thick as trees along all the
    rivers of America, and
      along the shores of the great lakes, and all over the
        prairies,
I will make inseparable cities with their arms about
      each other's necks,
    By the love of comrades,
       By the manly love of comrades.

For you these from me, O Democracy, to serve you ma
    femme!
For you, for you I am trilling these songs.

Our National Banner
July 4, 1876
Dexter Smith

O'er the high and o'er the lowly
Floats that banner bright and holy
   In the rays of Freedom's sun,
In the nation's heart embedded,
O'er our Union newly wedded,
   One in all, and all in one.

Let that banner wave forever,
May its lustrous stars fade never,
   Till the stars shall pale on high;
While there's right the wrong defeating,
While there's hope in true hearts beating,
   Truth and freedom shall not die.

As it floated long before us,
Be it ever floating o'er us,
   O'er our land from shore to shore;
There are freemen yet to wave it,
Millions who would die to save it,
   Wave it, save it, evermore.

Our Country
John Greenleaf Whittier
(1807–1892)

We give thy natal day to hope,
O Country of our love and prayer!
Thy way is down no fatal slope,
But up to freer sun and air.

Tried as by furnace-fires, and yet
By God's grace only stronger made,
In future tasks before thee set
Thou shalt not lack the old-time aid.

The fathers sleep, but men remain
As wise, as true, and brave as they;
Why count the loss and not the gain?
The best is that we have today.

Whate'er of folly, shame, or crime,
Within thy mighty bounds transpires,
With speed defying space and time,
Comes to us on the accusing wires;

While of thy wealth of noble deeds,
Thy homes of peace, thy votes unsold,
The love that pleads for human needs,
The wrong redressed, but half is told!

We read each felon's chronicle,
His acts, his words, his gallows-mood;
We know the single sinner well
And not the nine and ninety good.

Yet if, on daily scandals fed,
We seem at times to doubt thy worth,
We know thee still, when all is said,
The best and dearest spot on earth.

From the warm Mexic Gulf, or where
Belted with flowers Los Angeles
Basks in the semi-tropic air,
To where Katahdin's cedar trees

Are dwarfed and bent by Northern winds,
Thy plenty's horn is yearly filled;
Along, the rounding century finds
Thy liberal soil by free hands tilled.

A refuge for the wronged and poor,
Thy generous heart has borne the blame
That, with them, through thy open door,
The old world's evil outcasts came.

But, with thy just and equal rule,
And labor's need and breadth of lands,
Free press and rostrum, church and school,
Thy sure, if slow, transforming hands,

Shall mould even them to thy design,
Making a blessing of the ban;
And Freedom's chemistry combine
The alien elements of man.

The power that broke their prison bar
And set the dusky millions free,
And welded in the flame of war
The Union fast to Liberty;

Shall it not deal with other ills,
Redress the red man's grievance, break
The Circean cup which shames and kills,
And Labor full requital make?

Alone to such as fitly bear
Thy civic honors bid them fall?
And call thy daughters forth to share
The rights and duties pledged to all?

Give every child his right of school,
Merge private greed in public good,
And spare a treasury overfull
The tax upon a poor man's food?

No lack was in thy primal stock,
No weakling founders builded here;
Thine were the men of Plymouth Rock,
The Huguenot and Cavalier,

And they whose firm endurance gained
The freedom of the souls of men,
Whose hands, unstained with blood, maintained
The swordless commonwealth of Penn.

And thine shall be the power of all
To do the work which duty bids,
And make the people's council hall
As lasting as the Pyramids!

Well have thy later years made good
Thy brave-said word a century back,
The pledge of human brotherhood,
The equal claim of white and black.

That word still echoes round the world,
And all who hear it turn to thee,
And read upon thy flag unfurled
The prophecies of destiny.

Thy great world-lesson all shall learn,
The nations in thy school shall sit,
Earth's farthest mountain tops shall burn
With watch-fires from thy own uplit.

Great without seeking to be great
By fraud or conquest, rich in gold,
But richer in the large estate
Of virtue which thy children hold,

With peace that comes of purity
And strength to simple justice due,
So runs our loyal dream of thee;
God of our fathers! make it true.

O Land of lands! to thee we give
Our prayers, our hopes, our service free;
For thee thy sons shall nobly live,
And at thy need shall die for thee!

Freedom

Joel Barlow
(1754–1812)

Sun of the moral world; effulgent source
Of man's best wisdom and his steadiest force,
Soul-searching Freedom! here assume thy stand,
And radiate hence to every distant land;
Point out and prove how all the scenes of strife,
The shock of states, the impassion'd broils of life,
Spring from unequal sway; and how they fly
Before the splendor of thy peaceful eye;
Unfold at last the genuine social plan,
The mind's full scope, the dignity of man,
Bold nature bursting through her long disguise,
And nations daring to be just and wise.
Yes! righteous Freedom, heaven and earth and sea
Yield or withhold their various gifts for thee;
Protected Industry beneath thy reign
Leads all the virtues in her filial train;
Courageous Probity, with brow serene,
And Temperance calm presents her placid mien;
Contentment, Moderation, Labor, Art,
Mold the new man and humanize his heart:
To public plenty private ease dilates,
Domestic peace to harmony of states.
Protected Industry, careering far,
Detects the cause and cures the rage of war,
And sweeps, with forceful arm, to their last graves,
Kings from the earth and pirates from the waves.

The Great Land

WILLIAM ROSE BENET
(1886–1950)

Things that are good and great my land has given,
of thought and word and deed, and heart and mind.
Now that the seas run high and night is blind
I will steer with mine own kind by the stars of heaven.
Yes, now that day goes dark and night glows red
and a wind is blowing as over desert sand,
my trust is with her living and her dead,
My faith bestead in the love of my own land.

Words that were harsh enough we have used against
      her
who nourished all our rage or gentlest thought,
who roused, who nobly urged, who subtly taught,
while with our small concerns we recompensed
      her. . . .
Now, with high thunderheads and the storm breaking,
by day, by night, she is song along my blood,
the great land we have seldom understood.
Behind my opened eyes the tears are aching. . . .

So I say, lift up your hearts where you see her striding
helmed and harnessed into furious dawn,
with her sons that crowd around her striking on
till all portentous evil nowhere hiding;
and lift your voices too in a great shout
for victory's thunderclap on near occasions,
phalanx of eagles to free the captive nations,
stars in heaven no hurricane shall put out!

A Toast to the Flag

JOHN JAY DALY
(1888–1976)

Here's to the Red of it—
    There's not a thread of it,
    No, nor a shred of it
    In all the spread of it
        From foot to head
    But heroes bled for it,
    Faced steel and lead for it,
    Precious blood shed for it,
        Bathing it Red!

Here's to the White of it—
    Thrilled by the sight of it,
    Who knows the right of it
    But feels the might of it
        Through day and night?
    Womanhood's care for it
    Made manhood dare for it;
    Purity's pray'r for it
        Keeps it so White!

Here's to the Blue of it—
    Beauteous view of it,
    Heavenly hue of it,
    Star-spangled dew of it
        Sparkling anew;
    Diadems gleam for it,
    States stand supreme for it,
    Liberty's beam for it
        Brightens the Blue!

Here's to the Whole of it—
    Stars, stripes and pole of it,
    Body and soul of it,
    O, and the roll of it,
        Sun shining through;
    Hearts in accord for it
    Swear by the sword for it,
    Thanking the Lord for it,
        Red, White and Blue!

A Poem on the Industry of the United States of America
Excerpts
David Humphreys
(1753–1818)

Genius of Culture! thou, whose chaster taste
Can clothe with beauty ev'n the dreary waste;
Teach me to sing, what bright'ning charms unfold,
The bearded ears, that bend with more than gold;
How empire rises, and how morals spring,
From lowly labour, teach my lips to sing;
Exalt the numbers with thy gifts supreme,
Ennobler of the song, my guide and theme!

    Thou, toil! that mak'st, where our young empire
        grows,
The wilderness bloom beauteous as the rose,
Parent of wealth and joy! my nation's friend!
Be present, nature's rudest works to mend;
With all the arts of polish'd life to bless,
And half thy ills, Humanity! redress.
On this revolving day, that saw the birth
Of a whole nation glad th' astonished earth;
Thee I invoke to bless the recent reign
Of independence—but for thee how vain
Each fair advantage liberty has giv'n,
And all the copious bounties show'r'd by heav'n?
Hail, mighty pow'r! whose vivifying breath
Wakes vegetation on the barren heath;
Thou changest nature's face; thy influence such
Dark deserts brighten at thy glowing touch;
Creation springs where'er thy plough-share drives,
And the dead grain, an hundred fold, revives.
Thy voice, that dissipates the savage gloom,
Bade in the wild unwonted beauty bloom;
By thee and freedom guided, not in vain,
Our great fore-fathers dar'd the desert main;
O'er waves no keel had cut they found the shore,

Where desolation stain'd his steps with gore,

Th' immense of forest! where no tree was fell'd,
Where savage-men at midnight orgies yell'd;
Where howl'd round burning pyres each ravening
    beast,
As fiend-like forms devour'd their bloody feast,
And hoarse resounded o'er the horrid heath,
The doleful war-whoop, or the song of death.
Soon our progenitors subdu'd the wild,
And virgin nature, rob'd in verdure, smil'd.
They bade her fruits, through rifted rocks, from hills
Descend, misnam'd innavigable rills:
Bade houses, hamlets, towns, and cities rise,
And tow'rs and temples gild Columbian skies.
Success thence crown'd that bold, but patient band,
Whose undegen'rate sons possess the land;
Their great fore-fathers' principles avow,
And proudly dare to venerate the plough.

• • •

Say, ye who, not as tenants, till the soil,
The joys that freedmen find in rural toil?
In what blest spot, through all terraqueous space,
Exists a hardier or a happier race?
Ye bid your glebes with future germs rejoice,
And seeds that sleep inhum'd strait hear your voice.
How change the prospects at your blithe command!
Where weeds and brambles stood now flowrets stand.
How blooms the dell, as spreads the rippling rill,
While mottled cattle top the moving hill!
Bid marshall'd maize the tassell'd flag unfold,
And wheat-ears barb their glistening spears with gold:
In northern plains the orchard's produce glow,
Or with its beverage pure the press o'erflow;
In southern climes, beneath a fervid sky,
Savannas, green with rice, refresh the eye;
There, from th' adopted stranger-tree, despoil
The branch that cheers for peace, the fruit with oil.
O'er fens, reform'd, let verdant grass succeed
The blue-ting'd indigo—pestiferous weed!
Where dun, hoed fields, afford subsistence scant
For those who tend Tobago's luxury plant,
Bid other crops with brighter hues be crown'd,

And herb for beast, and bread for man abound.
With little fingers let the children cull,
Like flakes of snow, the vegetable wool;
Or nurse the *chrysalis* with mulberry leaves,
The *worm* whose silk the curious artist weaves:
Let buzzing bees display the winnowing wing,
Seek freshest flowers, and rifle all the spring:
Let brimming pails beside the heifers stand,
With milk and honey flow the happy land;
And turn the wildest growth to human use,
Ambrosial sugar find from maple-juice!

• • •

Ere ye begin to tread life's wider stage,
In manhood's prime, dear, interesting age!
Attend a time-taught bard, to toils inur'd,
With those bold chiefs whose blood your rights secur'd:
Ye junior patriots, listen! learn, my friends!
How much your lot on industry depends:
For God, a God of order, ne'er design'd,
Equal conditions for the human kind.
Equality of rights your bliss maintains,
While law protects what honest labour gains;
Your great exertions by restraint uncheck'd,
Your gen'rous heat undamp'd by cold neglect;
The wide career for freemen open lies,
Where wealth, and pow'r, and honour yield the prize.
Yet should dark discord's clouds your land o'ercast,
Lost is your freedom and your empire past.
Be union yours! To guard your union, heav'n
The general government, in *trust*, has giv'n:
Then, when ere long your fathers sleep in dust,
Preserve, like vestal fire, that *sacred* TRUST!

The Better Way

SUSAN COOLIDGE

(1835–1905)

Who serves his country best?
Not he who, for a brief and stormy space,
Leads forth her armies to the fierce affray.
Short is the time of turmoil and unrest,
Long years of peace succeed it and replace:
    There is a better way.

Who serves his country best?
Not he who guides her senates in debate,
And makes the laws which are her prop and stay;
Not he who wears the poet's purple vest
And sings her songs of love and grief and fate:
    There is a better way.

He serves his country best,
Who joins the tide that lifts her nobly on;
For speech has myriad tongues for every day,
And song but one; and law within the breast
Is stronger than the graven law on stone:
    This a better way.

He serves his country best
Who lives pure life, and doeth righteous deed,
And walks straight paths, however others stray,
And leaves his sons as uttermost bequest
A stainless record which all men may read:
    This is the better way.

No drop but serves the slowly lifting tide,
No dew but has an errand to some flower,
No smallest star but sheds some helpful ray,
And man by man, each giving to all the rest,
Makes the firm bulwark of the country's power:
    There is no better way.

Gettysburg Address
Speech at the Dedication of the National Cemetery at Gettysburg
November 19, 1863

ABRAHAM LINCOLN
(1809–1865)

Fourscore and seven years ago our fathers brought forth upon this continent a new nation, conceived in liberty, and dedicated to the proposition that all men are created equal. Now we are engaged in a great civil war, testing whether that nation, or any nation so conceived and so dedicated, can long endure. We are met on a great battlefield of that war. We have come to dedicate a portion of that field as a final resting-place for those who here gave their lives that that nation might live. It is altogether fitting and proper that we should do this. But in a larger sense we cannot dedicate, we cannot consecrate, we cannot hallow this ground. The brave men, living and dead, who struggled here, have consecrated it far above our poor power to add or detract. The world will little note, nor long remember, what we say here; but it can never forget what they did here. It is for us, the living, rather to be dedicated here to the unfinished work which they who fought here have thus far so nobly advanced. It is rather for us to be here dedicated to the great task remaining before us, that from these honored dead we take increased devotion to that cause for which they gave the last full measure of devotion; that we here highly resolve that these dead shall not have died in vain; that this nation, under God, shall have a new birth of freedom, and that government of the people, by the people, and for the people, shall not perish from the earth.

Booth Killed Lincoln
AMERICAN FOLK BALLAD

Wilkes Booth came to Washington, an actor great was
    he,
He played at Ford's Theater, and Lincoln went to see;
It was early in April, not many weeks ago,
The people of this fair city all gathered at the show.

The war it is all over, the people happy now,
And Abraham Lincoln arose to make his bow;
The people cheer him wildly, arising to their feet,
And Lincoln waving of his hand, he calmly takes his
    seat.

And while he sees the play go on, his thoughts are
    running deep,
His darling wife, close by his side, has fallen fast
    asleep;
From the box there hangs a flag, it is not the Stars
    and Bars,
The flag that holds within its folds bright gleaming
    Stripes and Stars.

J. Wilkes Booth he moves down the aisle, he had
    measured once before,
He passes Lincoln's bodyguard a-nodding at the door;
He holds a dagger in his right hand, a pistol in his left,
He shoots poor Lincoln in the temple, and sends his
    soul to rest.

The wife awakes from slumber, and screams in her
    rage,
Booth jumps over the railing, and lands him on the
    stage;
He'll rue the day, he'll rue the hour, as God him life
    shall give,
When Booth stood in the center stage, crying, "Tyrants
    shall not live!"

The people all excited then, cried everyone, "A hand!"
Cried all the people near, "For God's sake, save that
    man!"
Then Booth ran back with boot and spur across the
    backstage floor,
He mounts that trusty claybank mare, all saddled at
    the door.

J. Wilkes Booth, in his last play, all dressed in
    broadcloth deep,
He gallops down the alleyway, I hear those horses' feet;
Poor Lincoln then was heard to say, and all has gone to
    rest,
"Of all the actors in this town, I loved Wilkes Booth
    the best."

When Lilacs Last in the Dooryard Bloom'd

WALT WHITMAN

(1819–1892)

When lilacs last in the dooryard bloom'd,
And the great star early droop'd in the western sky in
    the night,
I mourn'd, and yet shall mourn with ever-returning
    spring.

Ever-returning spring, trinity sure to me you bring,
Lilac blooming perennial and drooping star in the
    west,
And thought of him I love.

O powerful western fallen star!
O shades of night—O moody, tearful night!
O great star disappear'd—O the black murk that hides
    the star!
O cruel hands that hold me powerless—O helpless soul
    of me!
O harsh surrounding cloud that will not free my soul.

• • •

Coffin that passes through lanes and streets,
Through day and night with the great cloud darkening
    the land,
With the pomp of the inloop'd flags with the cities
    draped in black,
With the show of the States themselves as of crape-
    veil'd women standing,
With processions long and winding and the flambeaus
    of the night,
With the countless torches lit, with the silent sea of
    faces and the unbared heads,
With the waiting depot, the arriving coffin, and the
    sombre faces,
With dirges through the night, with the thousand
    voices rising strong and solemn,

With all the mournful voices of the dirges pour'd
    around the coffin,
The dim-lit churches and the shuddering organs—
    where amid these your journey,
With the tolling tolling bells' perpetual clang,
Here, coffin that slowly passes,
I give you my sprig of lilac.

• • •

Cool Tombs

CARL SANDBURG
(1878–1967)

When Abraham Lincoln was shoveled into the tombs,
  he forgot the copperheads and the assassin . . . in
  the dust, in the cool tombs.

And Ulysses Grant lost all thought of con men and
    Wall Street, cash and collateral turned ashes . . . in
  the dust, in the cool tombs.

Pocahontas' body, lovely as a poplar, sweet as a red
    haw in November or a pawpaw in May, did she
    wonder? does she remember? . . . in the dust, in
  the cool tombs?

Take any streetful of people buying clothes and
    groceries, cheering a hero or throwing confetti and
    blowing tin horns . . . tell me if the lovers are
    losers . . . tell me if any get more than the lovers
    . . . in the dust . . . in the cool tombs.

I, Too

LANGSTON HUGHES
(1902–1967)

I, too, sing America.

I am the darker brother.
They send me to eat in the kitchen
When company comes,
But I laugh,
And eat well,
And grow strong.

Tomorrow,
I'll sit at the table
When company comes.
Nobody'll dare
Say to me,
"Eat in the kitchen,"
Then.

Besides,
They'll see how beautiful I am
And be ashamed—

I, too, am America.

The New Colossus

EMMA LAZARUS

(1849–1887)

Not like the brazen giant of Greek fame,
With conquering limbs astride from land to land;
Here at our sea-washed, sunset gates shall stand
A mighty woman with a torch, whose flame
Is the imprisoned lightning, and her name
Mother of Exiles. From her beacon hand
Glows world-wide welcome; her mild eyes command
The air-bridged harbor that twin cities frame.

"Keep, ancient lands, your storied pomp!" cries she
With silent lips. "Give me your tired, your poor,
Your huddled masses yearning to breathe free,
The wretched refuse of your teeming shore.
Send these, the homeless, tempest-tossed to me,
I lift my lamp beside the golden door."

America

CLAUDE McKAY

(1891–1948)

Although she feeds me bread of bitterness,
And sinks into my throat her tiger's tooth,
Stealing my breath of life, I will confess
I love this cultured hell that tests my youth!
Her vigor flows like tides into my blood,
Giving me strength erect against her hate.
Her bigness sweeps my being like a flood.
Yet as a rebel fronts a king in state,
I stand within her walls with not a shred
Of terror, malice, not a word or jeer.
Darkly I gaze into the days ahead,
And see her might and granite wonders there,
Beneath the touch of Time's unerring hand,
Like priceless treasures sinking in the sand.

This Land Is Your Land

WOODY GUTHRIE

(1912–1967)

This land is your land, this land is my land
From California to the New York island,
From the redwood forest to the Gulf Stream waters;
This land was made for you and me.

As I was walking that ribbon of highway
I saw above me that endless skyway;
I saw below me that golden valley;
This land was made for you and me.

I've roamed and rambled and I followed my footsteps
To the sparkling sands of her diamond deserts;
And all around me a voice was sounding;
This land was made for you and me.

One bright Sunday morning in the shadows of the
    steeple
By the Relief Office I seen my people;
As they stood there hungry, I stood there whistling:
This land was made for you and me.

When the sun came shining, and I was strolling,
And the wheat fields waving and the dust clouds
    rolling,
As the fog was lifting a voice was chanting:
This land was made for you and me.

Nobody living can ever stop me,
As I go walking that freedom highway;
Nobody living can ever make me turn back,
This land was made for you and me.

As I went walking, I saw a sign there,
And on the sign it said "No Trespassing."
But on the other side it didn't say nothing,
That side was made for you and me.

Words and music by Woody Guthrie. The Richman organization— © 1956 (renewed 1984), 1958 (renewed 1986) and 1970 Ludlow Music, Inc., New York, N.Y. Used by permission.

Land of the Free

ARTHUR NICHOLAS HOSKING

America, O Power benign, great hearts revere your
    name,
You stretch your hand to every land, to weak and
    strong the same;
You claim no conquest of the sea, nor conquest of the
    field,
But conquest for the rights of man, that despots all
    shall yield.

Chorus:
    America, fair land of mine, home of the just and
        true,
    All hail to thee, land of the free, and the Red-White-
        and-Blue.

America, staunch, undismayed, your spirit is our
    might:
No splendor falls on feudal walls upon your mountain's
    height,

But shafts of Justice pierce your skies to light the way
for all,
A world's great brotherhood of man, that cannot, must
not fall.

America, in God we trust, we fear no tyrant's horde:
There's light that leads toward better deeds than
conquest by the sword;
Yet our cause is just, if fight we must until the world
be free
Of every menace, breed, or caste that strikes at
Liberty.

America, home of the brave, our song in praise we
bring—
Where Stars and Stripes the winds unfurl, 'tis there
that tributes ring;
Our fathers gave their lives that we should live in
Freedom's light—
Our lives we consecrate to thee, our guide the Might of
Right.

There Is a Land

JAMES MONTGOMERY
(1771–1854)

There is a land, of every land the pride,
Beloved by Heaven o'er all the world beside;
Where brighter suns dispense serener light,
And milder moons imparadise the night:
A land of beauty, virtue, valor, truth,
Time-tutored age and love-exalted youth.
Where shall that land, that spot of earth, be found?
Art thou a man? A patriot? look around!
O! thou shalt find, howe'er thy footsteps roam,
That land thy country, and that spot thy home.

America Greets an Alien

AUTHOR UNKNOWN

Hail, guest! We ask not what thou art.
If friend, we greet thee hand and heart;
If stranger, such no longer be;
If foe, our love shall conquer thee.

Hail, Columbia

JOSEPH HOPKINSON

(1770–1842)

Hail! Columbia, happy land!
Hail! ye heroes, heaven-born band,
Who fought and bled in freedom's cause,
And when the storm of war was gone,
Enjoyed the peace your valor won;
Let independence be your boast,
Ever mindful what it cost,
Ever grateful for the prize,
Let its altar reach the skies.

Chorus:

> Firm, united let us be,
> Rallying round our liberty,
> As a band of brothers joined,
> Peace and safety we shall find.

Immortal patriots, rise once more!
Defend your rights, defend your shore;
Let no rude foe with impious hand,
Invade the shrine where sacred lies
Of toil and blood the well-earned prize;
While offering peace, sincere and just,
In heaven we place a manly trust,
That truth and justice will prevail,
And every scheme of bondage fail.

Sound, sound the trump of fame!
Let Washington's great name
Ring through the world with load applause!
Let every clime to freedom dear
Listen with a joyful ear;
With equal skill, with steady power,
He governs in the fearful hour
Of horrid war, or guides with ease
The happier time of honest peace.

Behold the chief, who now commands,
Once more to serve his country stands,
The rock on which the storm will beat!
But armed in virtue, firm and true,
His hopes are fixed on heaven and you.
When hope was sinking in dismay,
When gloom obscured Columbia's day,
His steady mind, from changes free,
Resolved on death or liberty.

No Land Like Ours

J. R. BARRICK

Though other lands may boast of skies
  Far deeper in their blue,
Where flowers in Eden's pristine dyes,
  Bloom with a richer hue;
And other nations pride in kings,
  And worship lordly powers;
Yet every voice of nature sings,
  There is no land like ours.

Though other scenes than such as grace
  Our forests, fields, and plains,
May lend the earth a sweeter face
  Where peace incessant reigns;
But dearest still to me the land
  Where sunshine cheers the hours,
For God hath shown, with his own hand,
  There is no land like ours!

Though other streams may softer flow
   In vales of classic bloom,
And rivers clear as crystal glow,
   That wear no tinge of gloom;
Though other mountains lofty look,
   And grand seem olden towers,
We see, as in an open book,
   There is no land like ours!

Though other nations boast of deeds
   That live in old renown,
And other peoples cling to creeds
   That coldly on us frown;
On pure religion, love, and law
   Are based our ruling powers—
The world but feels, with wondering awe,
   There is no land like ours!

Though other lands may boast their brave,
   Whose deeds are writ in fame,
Their heroes ne'er such glory gave
   As gilds our country's name;
Though others rush to daring deeds,
   Where the darkening war-cloud lowers,
Here, each alike for freedom bleeds—
   There is no land like ours!

Though other lands Napoleon
   And Wellington adorn,
America, her Washington,
   And later heroes born;
Yet Johnston, Jackson, Price, and Lee,
   Bragg, Buckner, Morgan towers,
With Beauregard, and Hood, and Bee—
   There is no land like ours!

The Prairies

WILLIAM CULLEN BRYANT

(1794–1878)

These are the gardens of the Desert, these
The unshorn fields, boundless and beautiful,
For which the speech of England has no name—
The Prairies. I behold them for the first,
And my heart swells, while the dilated sight
Takes in the encircling vastness. Lo! they stretch,
In airy undulations, far away,
As if the ocean, in his gentlest swell,
Stood still, with all his rounded billows fixed,
And motionless forever.—Motionless?—
No—they are all unchained again. The clouds
Sweep over with their shadows, and, beneath,
The surface rolls and fluctuates to the eye;
Dark hollows seem to glide along and chase
The sunny ridges. Breezes of the South!

Who toss the golden and the flame-like flowers,
And pass the prairie-hawk that, poised on high,
Flaps his broad wings, yet moves not—ye have played
Among the palms of Mexico and vines
Of Texas, and have crisped the limpid brooks,
That from the fountains of Sonora glide
Into the calm Pacific—have ye fanned
A nobler or a lovelier scene than this?
Man hath no power in all this glorious work:
The hand that built the firmament hath heaved
And smoothed these verdant swells, and sown their
    slopes
With herbage, planted them with island groves,
And hedged them round with forests. Fitting floor
For this magnificent temple of the sky—
With flowers whose glory and whose multitude
Rival the constellations! The great heavens
Seem to stoop down upon the scene in love,—
A nearer vault, and of a tenderer blue,
Than that which bends above our eastern hills.

As o'er the verdant waste I guide my steed,
Among the high rank grass that sweeps his sides
The hollow beating of his footstep seems
A sacrilegious sound. I think of those
Upon whose rest he tramples. Are they here—
The dead of other days?—and did the dust
Of these fair solitudes once stir with life
And burn with passion? Let the mighty mounds
That overlook the rivers, or that rise
In the dim forest crowded with old oaks,
Answer. A race, that long has passed away,
Built them;—a disciplined and populous race
Heaped, with long toil, the earth, while yet the Greek
Was hewing the Pentelicus to forms
Of symmetry, and rearing on its rock
The glittering Parthenon. These ample fields
Nourished their harvests, here their herds were fed,
When haply by their stalls the bison lowed,
And bowed his manèd shoulder to the yoke.
All day this desert murmured with their toils,
Till twilight blushed, and lovers walked, and wooed
In a forgotten language, and old tunes,
From instruments of unremembered form,
Gave the soft winds a voice. The red man came—
The roaming hunter tribes, warlike and fierce,

And the mound-builders vanished from the earth.
The solitude of centuries untold
Has settled where they dwelt. The prairie-wolf
Hunts in their meadows, and his fresh-dug den
Yawns by my path. The gopher mines the ground
Where stood their swarming cities. All is gone;
All—save the piles of earth that hold their bones,
The platforms where they worshipped unknown gods,
The barriers which they builded from the soil
To keep the foe at bay—till o'er the walls
The wild beleaguerers broke, and, one by one,
The strongholds of the plain were forced, and heaped
With corpses. The brown vultures of the wood
Flocked to those vast uncovered sepulchres,
And sat unscared and silent at their feast.

Haply some solitary fugitive,
Lurking in marsh and forest, till the sense
Of desolation and of fear became
Bitterer than death, yielded himself to die.
Man's better nature triumphed then. Kind words
Welcomed and soothed him; the rude conquerors
Seated the captive with their chiefs; he chose
A bride among their maidens, and at length
Seemed to forget—yet ne'er forgot—the wife
Of his first love, and her sweet little ones,
Butchered, amid their shrieks, with all his race.

Thus change the forms of being. Thus arise
Races of living things, glorious in strength,
And perish, as the quickening breath of God
Fills them, or is withdrawn. The red man, too,
Has left the blooming wilds he ranged so long,
And, nearer to the Rocky Mountains, sought
A wilder hunting-ground. The beaver builds
No longer by these streams, but far away,
On waters whose blue surface ne'er gave back
The white man's face—among Missouri's springs,
And pools whose issues swell the Oregon—
He rears his little Venice. In these plains
The bison feeds no more. Twice twenty leagues
Beyond remotest smoke of hunter's camp,
Roams the majestic brute, in herds that shake
The earth with thundering steps—yet here I meet
His ancient footprints stamped beside the pool.

Still this great solitude is quick with life.
Myriads of insects, gaudy as the flowers
They flutter over, gentle quadrupeds,
And birds, that scarce have learned the fear of man,
Are here, and sliding reptiles of the ground,
Startlingly beautiful. The graceful deer
Bounds to the wood at my approach. The bee,
A more adventurous colonist than man,
With whom he came across the eastern deep,
Fills the savannas with his murmurings,
And hides his sweets, as in the golden age,

Within the hollow oak. I listen long
To his domestic hum, and think I hear
The sound of that advancing multitude
Which soon shall fill these deserts. From the ground
Comes up the laugh of children, the soft voice
Of maidens, and the sweet and solemn hymn
Of Sabbath worshippers. The low of herds
Blends with the rustling of the heavy grain
Over the dark brown furrows. All at once
A fresher wind sweeps by, and breaks my dream,
And I am in the wilderness alone.

Reprinted by permission of Rowman & Littlefield, Totowa, N.J.

O Beautiful, My Country

Frederick L. Hosmer
(1840–1929)

"O beautiful, my country!"
 Be thine a nobler care,
Than all thy wealth of commerce,
 Thy harvest waving fair;
Be it thy pride to lift up
 The manhood of the poor;
Be thou to the oppressed
 Fair Freedom's open door.

For thee our fathers suffered,
 For thee they toiled and prayed;
Upon thy holy altar
 Their willing lives they laid.
Thou hast no common birthright;
 Grand memories on thee shine,
The blood of pilgrim nations,
 Commingled, flows in thine.

O beautiful, our country!
 Round thee in love we draw;
Thine is the grace of freedom,
 The majesty of law.
Be righteousness thy scepter,
 Justice thy diadem;
And on thy shining forehead
 Be peace the crowning gem.

America the Beautiful

KATHARINE LEE BATES

(1859–1929)

O beautiful for spacious skies,
  For amber waves of grain,
For purple mountain majesties
  Above the fruited plain!
    America! America!
  God shed His grace on thee
And crown thy good with brotherhood
  From sea to shining sea!

O beautiful for pilgrim feet,
  Whose stern, impassioned stress
A thoroughfare for freedom beat
  Across the wilderness!
    America! America!
  God mend thine every flaw,
Confirm thy soul in self-control,
  Thy liberty in law!

O beautiful for heroes proved
  In liberating strife,
Who more than self their country loved,
  And mercy more than life!
    America! America!
  May God thy gold refine
Till all success be nobleness,
  And every gain divine!

O beautiful for patriot dream
  That sees beyond the years
Thine alabaster cities gleam
  Undimmed by human tears!
    America! America!
  God shed His grace on thee
And crown thy good with brotherhood
  From sea to shining sea!

Shine, Republic

ROBINSON JEFFERS

(1887–1962)

The quality of these trees, green height; of the sky,
    shining, of water, a clear flow; of the rock,
    hardness
And reticence: each is noble in its quality. The love of
    freedom has been the quality of Western man.

There is a stubborn torch that flames from Marathon
    to Concord, its dangerous beauty binding three
    ages
Into one time; the waves of barbarism and civilization
    have eclipsed but have never quenched it.

For the Greeks the love of beauty, for Rome of ruling;
    for the present age the passionate love of
    discovery;
But in one noble passion we are one; and Washington,
    Luther, Tacitus, Aeschylus, one kind of man.

And you, America, that passion made you. You were
    not born to prosperity, you were born to love
    freedom.
You did not say "en masse," you said "independence."
    But we cannot have all the luxuries and freedom
    also.

Freedom is poor and laborious; that torch is not safe
    but hungry, and often requires blood for its fuel.
You will tame it against it burn too clearly, you will
    hood it like a kept hawk, you will perch it on the
    wrist of Caesar.

But keep the tradition, conserve the forms, the
    observances, keep the spot sore. Be great, carve
    deep your heel-harks.
The states of the next age will no doubt remember you,
    and edge their love of freedom with contempt of
    luxury.

The American Flag

JOSEPH RODMAN DRAKE

(1795–1820)

When Freedom from her mountain height
    Unfurled her standard to the air,
She tore the azure robe of night,
    And set the stars of glory there;
She mingled with its gorgeous dyes
The milky baldric of the skies,
And striped its pure, celestial white
With streakings of the morning light;
Then from his mansion in the sun
She called her eagle bearer down,
And gave into his mighty hand
The symbol of her chosen land.

Majestic monarch of the cloud!
    Who rear'st aloft thy regal form,
To hear the tempest-trumpings loud,
And see the lightning lances driven,
    When strive the warriors of the storm,
And rolls the thunder-drum of heaven—
Child of the sun! to thee 'tis given
    To guard the banner of the free,
To hover in the sulphur smoke,
To ward away the battle-stroke,
And bid its blendings shine afar,
Like rainbows on the cloud of war,
    The harbingers of victory!

Flag of the brave! thy folds shall fly,
The sign of hope and triumph high,
When speaks the signal trumpet tone,
And the long line comes gleaming on;
Ere yet the life-blood, warm and wet,
Has dimmed the glistening bayonet,
Each soldier eye shall brightly turn
To where thy sky-born glories burn,
And, as his springing steps advance,
Catch war and vengeance from the glance

And when the cannon-mouthings loud
Heave in wild wreaths the battle-shroud
And gory sabers rise and fall,
Like shoots of flame on midnight's pall;
Then shall thy meteor-glances glow,
    And cowering foes shall sink beneath
Each gallant arm that strikes below
    That lovely messenger of death.

Flag of the seas! on ocean wave
Thy stars shall glitter o'er the brave;
When death, careering on the gale,
Sweeps darkly round the bellied sail,
And frighted waves rush wildly back
Before the broadside's reeling rack,
Each dying wanderer of the sea
Shall look at once to heaven and thee,
And smile to see thy splendors fly
In triumph o'er his closing eye.

Flag of the free heart's hope and home,
    By angel hands to valor given;
Thy stars have lit the welkin dome,
    And all thy hues were born in heaven.
Forever float that standard sheet!
    Where breathes the foe but falls before us,
With Freedom's soil beneath our feet,
    And Freedom's banner streaming o'er us?

American Muse

STEPHEN VINCENT BENET

(1898–1943)

American muse, whose strong and diverse heart
So many men have tried to understand
But only made it smaller with their art,
Because you are as various as your land,

As mountainous-deep, as flowered with blue rivers,
Thirsty with deserts, buried under snows,
As native as the shape of Navajo quivers,
And native, too, as the sea-voyaged rose.

Swift runner, never captured or subdued,
Seven-branched elk beside the mountain stream,
That half a hundred hunters have pursued
But never matched their bullets with the dream,

Where the great huntsmen failed, I set my sorry
And mortal snare for your immortal quarry.

You are the buffalo-ghost, the broncho-ghost
With dollar-silver in your saddle-horn,
The cowboys riding in from Painted Post,
The Indian arrow in the Indian corn,

And you are the clipped velvet of the lawns
Where Shropshire grows from Massachusetts sods,
The grey Maine rocks—and the war-painted dawns
That break above the Garden of the Gods.

The prairie-schooners crawling toward the ore
And the cheap car, parked by the station-door.

Where the skyscrapers lift their foggy plumes
Of stranded smoke out of a stony mouth,
You are that high stone and its arrogant fumes,
And you are ruined gardens in the South

And bleak New England farms, so winter-white
Even their roofs look lonely, and the deep,
The middle grainland where the wind of night
Is like all blind earth sighing in her sleep.

A friend, an enemy, a sacred hag
With two tied oceans in her medicine-bag.

They tried to fit you with an English song
And clip your speech into the English tale.
But, even from the first, the words went wrong.
The catbird pecked away the nightingale.

The homesick men begot high-cheekboned things
Whose wit was whittled with a different sound,
And Thames and all the rivers of the kings
Ran into Mississippi and were drowned.

They planted England with a stubborn trust,
But the cleft dust was never English dust.

Stepchild of every exile from content
And all the disavouched, hard-bitten pack
Shipped overseas to steal a continent
With neither shirts nor honor to their back,

Pimping grandee and rump-faced regicide,
Apple-cheeked younkers from a windmill-square,
Puritans stubborn as the nails of Pride,
Rakes from Versailles and thieves from County Clare,

The black-robed priests who broke their hearts in vain
To make you God and France or God and Spain.

These were your lovers in your buckskin-youth,
And each one married with a dream so proud
He never knew it could not be the truth
And that he coupled with a girl of cloud.

And now to see you is more difficult yet
Except as an immensity of wheel
Made up of wheels, oiled with inhuman sweat
And glittering with the heat of ladled steel.

All these you are, and each is partly you,
And none is false, and none is wholly true.

The Kansas Emigrants
July, 1854
JOHN GREENLEAF WHITTIER
(1807–1892)

We cross the prairie as of old
   The pilgrims crossed the sea,
To make the West, as they the East,
   The homestead of the free!

We go to rear a wall of men
   On Freedom's southern line,
And plant beside the cotton-tree
   The rugged Northern pine!

We're flowing from our native hills
   As our free rivers flow:
The blessing of our Mother-land
   Is on us as we go.

We go to plant her common schools
   On distant prairie swells,
And give the Sabbaths of the wild
   The music of her bells.

Upbearing, like the Ark of old,
  The Bible in our van,
We go to test the truth of God
  Against the fraud of man.

No pause, nor rest, save where the streams
  That feed the Kansas run,
Save where our Pilgrim gonfalon
  Shall flout the setting sun!

We'll tread the prairie as of old
  Our fathers sailed the sea,
And make the West, as they the East,
  The homestead of the free!

Prairie Birth

GRACE STONE COATES
(1881–?)

I was born on the prairie:
  I know how a partridge rises
Like a bullet out of the grain fields.
  I have watched the coveys of quail
Running along the road
  In front of a loaded wagon
And the wagons hurrying to the barn
  Ahead of the rattling hail.

Here the valleys lift
  Toward pine-swept peaks above them;
I hold my peace when their dwellers
  Disparage the level sod.
Canyon and cliff are vast;
  My heart is glad that men love them.
But no less for me on the prairie
  Has rested the hand of God.

Northbound
LARRY RUBIN
(1930-   )

Leaving tropic parallels
For Northern desolation,
I like to trace declining trends
In Southern vegetation.

The palm trees are the first to go—
by Carolina, lost—
Like youthful flarings, much too frail
To stand maturing frost.

Next, the live oak; then resinous pine;
Then wild savannahs fade,
Absented by climatic rules
As stern as latitude.

Transition ends on Maine's rock hills,
Beyond thick glades and loam;
An ancient thorn tree, twisted skies
Welcome the traveler home.

Plain-Chant for America

KATHERINE GARRISON CHAPIN
(1890–1977)

For the dream unfinished
Out of which we came,
We stand together,
While a hemisphere darkens
And the nations flame.

Our earth has been hallowed
With death for freedom;
Our walls have been hallowed
With freedom's thought.

Concord, Valley Forge, Harpers Ferry
Light up with their flares
Our sky of doubt.

We fear tyranny as our hidden enemy:
The black-shirt cruelty, the goose-step mind.

No dark signs close the doors of our speaking,
No bayonets bar the door to our prayers,
No gun butts shadow our children's eyes.

If we have failed—lynchings in Georgia,
Justice in Massachusetts undone,
The bloody fields of South Chicago—
Still a voice from the bruised and the battered
Speaks out in the light of a free sun.

Saying, "Tell them again, say it, America;
Say it again till it splits their ears:
Freedom is salt in our blood and its bone shape;
If freedom fails, we'll fight for more freedom—
This is the land, and these are the years!
When freedom's a whisper above their ashes
An obsolete word cut on their graves,
When the mind has yielded its last resistance,
And the last free flag is under the waves—

"Let them remember that here on the western
Horizon a star, once acclaimed, has not set;
And the strength of a hope, and the shape of a vision
Died for and sung for and fought for,
And worked for,
Is living yet."

I Am What You Make Me
(The Flag Speaks)
Franklin K. Lane

I am whatever you make me, nothing more.
I am your belief in yourself, your dream of what a
     people may become.
I live a changing life, a life of moods and passions, of
     heartbreaks and tired muscles.
Sometimes I am strong with pride, when workmen do
     an honest piece of work,
Sometimes I droop, for then purpose has gone from
     me, and cynically I play the coward;
But always I am all that you hope to be, and have the
     courage to try for.
I am song and fear, struggle and panic, and ennobling
     hope.
I am the day's work of the weakest man, and the
     largest dream of the most daring.
I am what you make me, nothing more.

I swing before your eyes as a bright gleam of color,
A symbol of yourself,
A pictured suggestion of that big thing which makes
     this nation.
My stars and stripes are your dream and your labors,
They are bright with cheer, brilliant with courage,
     firm with faith,
Because you have made them so out of your hearts

The Soldier
ROBERT FROST
(1874–1963)

He is that fallen lance that lies as hurled,
That lies unlifted now, come dew, come rust,
But still lies pointed as it plowed the dust.
If we who sight along it round the world,
See nothing worthy to have been its mark,
It is because like men we look too near,
Forgetting that as fitted to the sphere,
Our missiles always make too short an arc.
They fall, they rip the grass, they intersect
The curve of earth, and striking, break their own;
They make us cringe for metal-point on stone.
But this we know, the obstacle that checked
And tripped the body, shot the spirit on
Further than target ever showed or shone.

Armistice Day

John Freeman
(1885-?)

Birds stayed not their singing,
The heart its beating,
The blood its steady coursing
  The child in the dark womb
Stirred; dust settled in the tomb.

Old wounds were still smarting,
Echoes were hollow-sounding,
New desires still upspringing.
  No silent Armistice might stay
Life and Death wrangling in the old way.

Earth's pulse still was beating,
The bright stars circling;
Only our tongues were hushing.
  While Time ticked silent on, men drew
A deeper breath than passion knew.

November 1918

JOSEPH MILLS HANSON

(b. 1876)

November's misty sunshine on the streets of Paris lay;
The colors of all the Allies from window and wall were
　　gay;
There was laughter and joy in plenty, as, under the
　　autumn sky
I saw, through the Arch of Triumph, the Stars and
　　Stripes go by.

By a band of martial music the fluttering flag was led,
And a column of drab-clad soldiers with rapid
　　rhythmic tread;
And the passing throng of Paris stood rigid, with eyes
　　aflame
As under the Arch of Triumph my country's banner
　　came.

And the hush that was on the people found echo in my
　　breast;
It beat with a deep thanksgiving that our flag from
　　the golden west,
In the fight for human freedom had borne so brave a
　　share,
And wherever the wind unfurls it, the heads of men
　　are bare;

That the lads of our drab-clad armies at Trugny and
　　Montfaucon
On the flaming slopes of Mezy, in the hell of the deep
　　Argonne,
Had fought with as fine a courage for the lands where
　　the Hun had trod
As the men of the elder decades who fought for their
　　native sod.

For now, through the misty sunshine that veiled the
    queenly town
The bronze men over the archway on the passing flag
    looked down—
The men of Lodi and Jena, and it seemed that their
    haughty glance
Said: "Flag of the Great Republic, thou, too, art at
    home in France;

Thou has won the right in glory on the fields where
    thy arms have gleamed
To stand with our own Tricolor in the hearts of a race
    redeemed."
Then the martial music quickened, and a flame on the
    misty sky—
From the shade of the Arch of Triumph the Stars and
    Stripes went by.

The Yankee's Return
from Camp
EDWARD BANGS
(c.1758-?)

Father and I went down to camp,
    Along with Captain Gooding,
And there we see the men and boys,
    As thick as hasty pudding.

Chorus
    Yankee Doodle, keep it up,
        Yankee Doodle, dandy,
    Mind the music and the step,
        And with the girls be handy.

And there we see a thousand men,
    As rich as 'Squire David;
And what they wasted every day
    I wish it could be saved. . . .

And there we see a swamping gun,
    Large as a log of maple,
Upon a deucèd little cart,
    A load for father's cattle.

And every time they shoot it off,
    It takes a horn of powder,
And makes a noise like father's gun,
    Only a nation louder. . . .

I see a little barrel, too,
    The heads were made of leather,
They knocked upon 't with little clubs
    And called the folks together.

And there was Captain Washington,
    And gentlefolks about him,
They say he's grown so tarnal proud
    He will not ride without 'em.

He got him on his meeting clothes,
    Upon a strapping stallion,
He set the world along in rows,
    In hundreds and in millions. . . .

I see another snarl of men
    A-digging graves, they told me,
So tarnal long, so tarnal deep,
    They 'tended they should hold me.

It scared me so, I hooked it off,
    Nor stopped, as I remember,
Nor turned about, till I got home,
    Locked up in mother's chamber.

When Johnny Comes Marching Home

Patrick Sarsfield Gilmore
(1829–1892)

When Johnny comes marching home again,
  Hurrah! hurrah!
We'll give him a hearty welcome then,
  Hurrah! hurrah!
The men will cheer, the boys will shout,
The ladies, they will all turn out,
  And we'll all feel gay,
When Johnny comes marching home.

The old church-bell will peal with joy,
  Hurrah! hurrah!
To welcome home our darling boy,
  Hurrah! hurrah!
The village lads and lasses say,
With roses they will strew the way;
  And we'll all feel gay,
When Johnny comes marching home.

Get ready for the jubilee,
  Hurrah! hurrah!
We'll give the hero three times three,
  Hurrah! hurrah!
The laurel-wreath is ready now
To place upon his loyal brow,
  And we'll all feel gay,
When Johnny comes marching home.

Let love and friendship on that day,
  Hurrah! hurrah!
Their choicest treasures then display,
  Hurrah! hurrah!
And let each one perform some part,
To fill with joy the warrior's heart;
  And we'll all feel gay,
When Johnny comes marching home.

In Flanders Fields

JOHN McCRAE
(1872-1918)

In Flanders fields the poppies blow
Between the crosses, row on row,
   That mark our place; and in the sky
   The larks, still bravely singing, fly
Scarce heard amid the guns below.

We are the Dead. Short days ago
We lived, felt dawn, saw sunset glow,
   Loved and were loved, and now we lie
   In Flanders fields.

Take up our quarrel with the foe:
To you from failing hands we throw
   The torch; be yours to hold it high.
   If ye break faith with us who die
We shall not sleep, though poppies grow
   In Flanders fields.

America's Answer

R. W. LILLIARD

Rest ye in peace, ye Flanders dead.
The fight that ye so bravely led
We've taken up. And we will keep
True faith with you who lie asleep
With each a cross to mark his bed,
   In Flanders fields.

Fear not that ye have died for naught.
The torch ye threw to us we caught.
Ten million hands will hold it high,
And Freedom's light shall never die!
We've learned the lesson that ye taught
   In Flanders fields.

How Shall We Honor Them?

AUTHOR UNKNOWN

How shall we honor them, our Deathless Dead?
With strew of laurel and the stately tread?
With blaze of banners brightening overhead?
Nay, not alone these cheaper praises bring:
They will not have this easy honoring.

• • •

How shall we honor them, our Deathless Dead?
How keep their mighty memories alive?
In him who feels their passion, they survive!
Flatter their souls with deeds, and all is said!

The Unknown Soldier

BILLY ROSE

(1899–1966)

There's a graveyard near the White House
   Where the Unknown Soldier lies,
And the flowers there are sprinkled
   With the tears from mother's eyes.

I stood there not so long ago
   With roses for the brave,
And suddenly I heard a voice
   Speak from out the grave:

"I am the Unknown Soldier,"
   The spirit voice began,
"And I think I have the right
   To ask some questions man to man.

"Are my buddies taken care of?
   Was their victory so sweet?
Is that big reward you offered
   Selling pencils on the street?

"Did they really win the freedom
   They battled to achieve?
Do you still respect that Croix de Guerre
   Above that empty sleeve?

"Does a gold star in the window
   Now mean anything at all?
I wonder how my old girl feels
   When she hears a bugle call.

"And that baby who sang
   'Hello, Central, give me no man's land'—
Can they replace her daddy
   With a military band?

"I wonder if the profiteers
  Have satisfied their greed?
I wonder if a soldier's mother
  Ever is in need?

"I wonder if the kings, who planned it all
  Are really satisfied?
They played their game of checkers
  And eleven million died.

"I am the Unknown Soldier
  And maybe I died in vain,
But if I were alive and my country called,
  I'd do it all over again."

The Old Flag

H. C. BUNNER
(1855–1896)

Off with your hat as the flag goes by!
  And let the heart have its say;
You're man enough for a tear in your eye
  That you will not wipe away.

You're man enough for a thrill that goes
  To your very finger tips;
Ay! the lump just then in your throat that rose
  Spoke more than your parted lips.

Lift up the boy on your shoulder high,
  And show him the faded shred;
Those stripes would be red as the sunset sky
  If death could have dyed them red.

Off with your hat as the flag goes by!
  Uncover the youngster's head,
Teach him to hold it holy and high
  For the sake of its sacred dead.

Prayer for America

PETER MARSHALL

(1902–1949)

Oh, God on high, we pray to Thee:
Preserve this land of liberty,
The land where heroes fought and died
To stem oppression's rising tide,
The only land upon the earth
Where all may rise above their birth,

Whose people seek to keep these shores
Immune from class and racial wars,
Whose Eagle's not a bird of prey,
But one who guards us night and day.
Protect us from dissension's hates—
Lord bless our great United States.

Our Flag

MARK TWAIN

(1835–1910)

And our flag—another pride of ours, our chiefest!
When we have seen it in far lands—glimpsing it
unexpectedly in that strange sky, waving its welcome
and benediction to us—we have caught our breaths,
and uncovered our heads, and couldn't speak, for a
moment, for the thought of what it was to us and the
great ideals it stood for.

Tribute to America

PERCY BYSSHE SHELLEY

(1792–1822)

There is a people mighty in its youth,
   A land beyond the oceans of the west,
Where, though with rudest rites, Freedom and Truth
   Are worshipt. From a glorious mother's breast,
   Who, since high Athens fell, among the rest
Sate like the Queen of Nations, but in woe,
   By inbred monsters outraged and opprest,
Turns to her chainless child for succor now,
It draws the milk of Power in Wisdom's fullest flow

That land is like an eagle, whose young gaze
   Feeds on the noontide beam, whose golden plume
Floats moveless on the storm, and on the blaze
   Of sunrise gleams when Earth is wrapt in gloom;
   An epitaph of glory for thy tomb
Of murdered Europe may thy fame be made,
   Great People! As the sands shalt thou become;
Thy growth is swift as morn when night must fade;
The multitudinous Earth shall sleep beneath thy shade.

Yes, in the desert, there is built a home
   For Freedom! Genius is made strong to rear
The monuments of man beneath the dome
   Of a new Heaven; myriads assemble there
   Whom the proud lords of man, in rage or fear,
Drive from their wasted homes. The boon I pray
   Is this—that Cythna shall be convoyed there,—
Nay, start not at the name—America!

I Have a Dream

MARTIN LUTHER KING, JR.

(1929–1968)

Excerpt from the address at the Lincoln Memorial during the March on Washington, August 28, 1963.

I say to you today, my friends, so even though we face the difficulties of today and tomorrow, I still have a dream. It is a dream deeply rooted in the American dream. I have a dream that one day this nation will rise up and live out the true meaning of its creed, "We hold these truths to be self-evident, that all men are created equal." I have a dream that one day on the red hills of Georgia sons of former slaves and the sons of former slave-owners will be able to sit down together at the table of brotherhood. I have a dream that one day even the state of Mississippi, a state sweltering with the heat of injustice, sweltering with the heat of oppression, will be transformed into an oasis of freedom and justice. I have a dream that my four little children will one day live in a nation where they will not be judged by the color of their skin but by the content of their character.

I HAVE A DREAM TODAY!

I have a dream that one day down in Alabama— with its vicious racists, with its governor having his lips dripping with the words of interposition and nullification, one day right there in Alabama little black boys and black girls will be able to join hands with little white boys and white girls as sisters and brothers.

I HAVE A DREAM TODAY!

I have a dream that one day every valley shall be exalted, every hill and mountain shall be made low. The rough places will be made plain, and the crooked places will be made straight, "and the glory of the Lord shall be revealed, and all flesh shall see it together."

This is our hope. This is the faith that I go back to the South with. With this faith we will be able to hew out of the mountain of despair a stone of hope. With this faith we will be able to transform the jangling discords of our nation into a beautiful symphony of brotherhood. With this faith we will be able to work together, to pray together, to struggle together, to go to jail together, to stand up for freedom together, knowing that we will be free one day. This will be the day when all of God's children will be able to sing with new meaning, "My country, 'tis of thee, sweet land of liberty, of thee I sing. Land where my father died, land of the pilgrim's pride, from every mountainside, let freedom ring." And if America is to be a great nation, this must become true.

So let freedom ring from the prodigious hilltops of New Hampshire; let freedom ring from the mighty mountains of New York; let freedom ring from the heightening Alleghenies of Pennsylvania; let freedom ring from the snow-capped Rockies of Colorado; let freedom ring from the curvaceous slopes of California. But not only that. Let freedom ring from Stone Mountain of Georgia; let freedom ring from Lookout Mountain of Tennessee; let freedom ring from every hill and molehill of Mississippi. "From every mountain side. Let freedom ring."

And when this happens, and when we allow freedom to ring, when we let it ring from every village and every hamlet, from every state and every city, we will be able to speed up that day when all of God's children, black men and white men, Jews and Gentiles, Protestants and Catholics, will be able to join hands and sing in the words of the old Negro spiritual: "Free at last. Free at last. Thank God Almighty, we are free at last."

Index

135

PROSE

Index of Authors